Comments on o

MW01254260

"*Tightly written volumes filled with lots of wit and humour about famous and infamous Canadians.*"
Eric Shackleton, *The Globe and Mail*

"*The heightened sense of drama and intrigue, combined with a good dose of human interest is what sets* Amazing Stories *apart.*"
Pamela Klaffke, *Calgary Herald*

"*This is popular history as it should be... For this price, buy two and give one to a friend.*"
Terry Cook, a reader from Ottawa, on **Rebel Women**

"*Glasner creates the moment of the explosion itself in graphic detail...she builds detail upon gruesome detail to create a convincingly authentic picture.*"
Peggy McKinnon, *The Sunday Herald,* on **The Halifax Explosion**

"*It was wonderful...I found I could not put it down. I was sorry when it was completed.*"
Dorothy F. from Manitoba on **Marie-Anne Lagimodière**

"*Stories are rich in description, and bristle with a clever, stylish realness.*"
Mark Weber, *Central Alberta Advisor,* on **Ghost Town Stories II**

"*A compelling read. Bertin...has selected only the most intriguing tales, which she narrates with a wealth of detail.*"
Joyce Glasner, *New Brunswick Reader,* on **Strange Events**

"*The resulting book is one readers will want to share with all the women in their lives.*"
Lynn Martel, *Rocky Mountain Outlook,* on **Women Explorers**

Battle at Leliefontaine at the Komati River - RC Dragoons

CANADA'S SOLDIERS IN SOUTH AFRICA

Tales from the Boer War, 1899–1902

Defeated at Hartis River — 33 Killed Transvaal

John Boileau

Boer War Began

Oct 12/1899

Finished 1902

MILITARY HISTORY

James Lorimer & Company Ltd., Publishers
Toronto

Defeated at the Modder River (Parradeberg) Feb 18/1900 11 Killed — Orange Free State

Copyright © 2011 by John Boileau

James Lorimer & Company Ltd., Publishers acknowledges the support of the Ontario Arts Council. We acknowledge the financial support of the Government of Canada through the Canada Book Fund for our publishing activities. We acknowledge the support of the Canada Council for the Arts, which last year invested $20.1 million in writing and publishing throughout Canada. We acknowledge the Government of Ontario through the Ontario Media Development Corporation's Ontario Book Initiative.

ONTARIO ARTS COUNCIL
CONSEIL DES ARTS DE L'ONTARIO

Canada Council
for the Arts

Library and Archives Canada Cataloguing in Publication

Boileau, John
Canada's soldiers in South Africa : tales from the Boer War, 1899-1902 / John Boileau.

(Amazing stories)
Includes bibliographical references and index.
Issued also in an electronic format.
ISBN 978-1-55277-725-1

1. South African War, 1899-1902--Participation, Canadian.
2. Canada. Canadian Army--History--South African War, 1899-1902. I. Title. II. Series: Amazing stories (Toronto, Ont.)

DT1913.C3B64 2011   968.04'840971   C2011-900772-X

James Lorimer & Company Ltd., Publishers
317 Adelaide Street West, Suite 1002
Toronto, ON, Canada
M5V 1P9
www.lorimer.ca

Printed in Canada

FSC
www.fsc.org
MIX
Paper from
responsible sources
FSC® C016245

To the memory of the officers and men who fought in South Africa with the Royal Canadian Dragoons and Strathcona's Horse—the two regiments in which I served during my army career.

Contents

SOUTHERN AFRICA 1899 – 1902

GERMAN
SOUTH
WEST
AFRICA

BECHUANALAND

TRANSVAAL

Middelburg
Lydenburg
X
• Belfast

Pretoria ★
Johannesburg •
Mafeking •
Driekuil
•
X Leliefontein
• Carolina
• Frederikstad
Klerksdorp
X Boschbult
• Standerton

Vredefort
Newcastle •
Kroonstad •

ORANGE FREE STATE
Harrismith •
• Ladysmith
Kimberley •
Graspan
X Paardeberg
Douglas •
Bloemfontein ★
Sunnyside X
NATAL
Belmont •
• Ramdam
Kenhardt •
Orange •
River
Station
Springfontein •
BASUTOLAND
Durban

Van Wyks Vlei •

Carnarvon •
• De Aar

CAPE COLONY

LEGEND
• Capital Cities
• Other Cities & Towns
X Canadian Battle Sites

★ Capetown
• Rondebosch
• Wynberg

Prologue

Shortly before dawn four soldiers of the Canadian Mounted Rifles reluctantly rolled out of their blankets to face another chilly South African morning. It looked like it was going to be another dry and dusty June day.

After a hasty breakfast of coffee and hardtack, the tough ranchers from the Pincher Creek area of Alberta rode out from their camp at a small train siding on the main rail line. On the gently rolling prairie, or veldt, as it was called in South Africa, three kilometres south of the train station, they set up a temporary observation post. Their job was to guard the rail line from attack from the Boers—farmers who had taken up arms against the British.

That morning about four hundred Boers attacked the main camp. When sixty of them tried to circle around, they ran into the observation post south of the station. Corporal James Morden—who was known as the best rancher in Pincher Creek—and his three men opened fire. Their only protection was the low railway bed.

Private Henry Miles suffered a hand wound almost immediately. Morden sent him back to the station with the horses, with orders to tell the main body that the small post would hold out.

Shortly after his brother left, a Boer bullet shattered Acting Corporal Thomas Miles's shoulder. Lying against a clump of grass to staunch the bleeding, Miles directed the fire of his two comrades.

Private Robert Kerr was shot next. Although wounded in the side, he continued to fire until he was hit in the heart. Morden fought on alone. Then a bullet through his brain silenced him forever.

Faced with such surprisingly stiff opposition from the Canadians—most men would have surrendered in a similar situation—the Boers called off their attack.

Chapter 1
Canada Answers the Call

In the early morning hours of October 12, 1899, soldiers of the citizens' militia of the little independent Boer republics of the Orange Free State and the Transvaal advanced south and east into the British territories of Cape Colony and Natal at the southern tip of Africa. In doing so, a handful of rugged farmers directly challenged Great Britain, the mightiest nation on earth at the time. The Boer, or South African, War had begun. It was the last of Queen Victoria's "little wars."

The Boers were descendants of Dutch farmers who came to the southern tip of Africa in the seventeenth century, when the area was a colony of Holland. Although Britain had acquired the region in 1815, the Boers remained fiercely independent and did not take kindly to outsiders meddling in their affairs, especially the British, the world's inveterate meddlers at the time.

In frustration, particularly with Britain's abolition of slavery in the early 1830s, the Boers made an epic long march, known as the "Great Trek," into the vast, empty interior of the continent, an area few whites had seen. Families and neighbours banded together and set out in long, slow columns of ox-drawn wagons, accompanied by their black slaves and animal herds. Some Boers crossed the Orange River and founded the Orange Free State, while others went further north, across the Vaal River and established the Transvaal. Many died en route.

The discovery of diamonds in 1867 and gold in 1884 in the Transvaal caused foreigners, known as *Uitlanders* (outsiders)—the majority of them British—to descend upon the area in hordes, bent on making their fortune. As the large foreign population grew, it soon outnumbered the Boers.

Uitlanders demanded the same rights as Boer citizens, including an entitlement to vote, a goal that the British also supported. Matters came to a head in 1898, when Britain attempted to force the Transvaal to permit Uitlanders to vote. Negotiations failed to resolve the issue.

Both sides began preparations for war. The tough, unbending president of the Transvaal, Paul Kruger, then issued an ultimatum for Britain to withdraw her troops from his borders. When the British refusal came in less than forty-eight hours, the Boers immediately invaded.

The Boers were not the easy opponents the British expected. They did not have a regular, permanent army, but a forty- to forty-five-thousand-man citizens' militia organized loosely as mounted infantry into groups called commandos. They had no uniforms, pay, or military training. But they were exceptionally mobile on horseback and skilled in the bushcraft of the "veldt," as the high South African plains were called.

The Boers were also expert marksmen armed with modern, high-powered Mauser rifles, and possessed a small, well-equipped, professional artillery force of about sixty guns. Unlike the British, they fought spread out so as not to offer a mass target to the enemy. They fired from behind cover at long ranges; when larger British forces got close, they simply mounted their horses and rode off, easily outdistancing the infantry. Such tactics were necessary to preserve the Boers' slender manpower resources, and they worked amazingly well.

Above all, the Boers were a rugged people, who were fighting on familiar terrain and used to living off the land. They also possessed a strong belief in being God's chosen people and in the righteousness of their cause.

Although the war was fought in Africa, neither the Boers nor the British employed local native levies to assist them;

there was a tacit agreement between both sides that this was to be a white man's war. Boers and British considered it inadvisable to use any but white soldiers in a war fought between white men in a country where—given the prejudices of the time—the utilization of black soldiers would cause enormous difficulties. Similarly, the British did not employ natives from their vast and experienced Indian Army except as non-combatants.

The Boer War had an immediate effect on Canada. Most Canadians had an opinion about it, and the majority were in favour of dispatching a contingent to help the British. Nearly all French Canadians, on the other hand, stood out as the most vocal opponents of a Canadian contribution.

The charming and charismatic Sir Wilfrid Laurier, the country's first French-Canadian prime minister, opposed sending his countrymen to fight in a war in which he felt no Canadian interests were at stake. But Laurier seriously misjudged the mood of the country. Throughout the summer and fall of 1899, partisan newspapers whipped the public into a frenzy of Boer-bashing. Laurier finally acquiesced to public opinion—at least that of English Canada. In mid-October, he offered to send an infantry battalion of one thousand volunteers to South Africa. The British promptly accepted.

To meet the end-of-October embarkation deadline imposed by the British, Ottawa's Department of Militia and Defence swung into action. There were a mere sixteen days to recruit, examine, organize, clothe, equip, concentrate, and dispatch the troops to South Africa—as well as to resolve political squabbles over the appointment of officers.

Recruiting started immediately for eight 125-man infantry companies: at Victoria, Vancouver, and Winnipeg for A Company; London for B; Toronto for C; Ottawa and Kingston for D; Montreal for E; Quebec for F; Saint John and Charlottetown for G; and Halifax for H.

Large numbers of prospective recruits responded. They had to be between twenty-two and forty years old, stand at least five feet six inches tall, and sign up for six months service, or one year if required. Rates of pay ranged from 50¢ a day for a private up to $4.75 a day for a lieutenant-colonel. Some militia officers were so keen to join that they served as privates.

Clothing consisted of three uniforms: two of rifle-green serge and one of khaki canvas. Headdress was a white pith helmet and khaki felt field cap. The sturdy Canadian-made black leather ankle boots proved to be better than the ones the British had.

Both officers and men wore distinctive Canadian Oliver pattern equipment, including cross-belt, ammunition pouch, and haversack. In addition, officers wore Sam Browne belts. Their uniforms were similar to the men's, but of better cut and material.

Everyone was also given an ammunition bandolier, water bottle, emergency food ration, and a brown leather valise for blankets. Soldiers were armed with the new ten-shot Lee-Enfield rifle, a bolt-operated weapon that fired a .303-calibre bullet. Officers were issued swords and Colt revolvers.

In late October, the soldiers marched through cheering crowds in their recruitment cities to train stations for the trip to the concentration point at Quebec. There, weapons, equipment, ammunition, clothing, camp stores, and other supplies were issued to the men or stowed aboard the ship that was to carry them to South Africa.

On Monday morning, October 30, more than a thousand soldiers from across Canada stood at attention on the Esplanade at Quebec City, awaiting the arrival of dignitaries. It was a cold and grey fall day, made all the worse by rain and hail. Everyone from the lowliest private to the troops' commander was quickly—and completely—soaked.

Despite the rain, most of the men were well aware of the significance of the occasion: they were members of the first Canadian military unit ever to be sent overseas. The 2nd (Special Service) Battalion, Royal Canadian Regiment—usually known as 2 RCR or simply the RCR—had been created almost overnight.

The contrast with the climate of the country to which they were going, generally assumed to be hot and dry, could not have been more obvious. Hot and dry was the exact opposite of the weather on this wretched October day, and the driving rain and hail only served to emphasize the difference.

The men—most of them had to remind themselves that they were soldiers now—paraded self-consciously in their new rifle-green serge uniforms and white helmets. Their once-pristine uniforms, fresh from the manufacturer, were now thoroughly waterlogged. Despite the unpleasant weather, a crowd estimated at as many as fifty thousand jostled for places to watch the military spectacle unfold before them.

The soldiers were a magnificent lot, described by the newspapers of the day in such grandiose terms as "representatives of ideal Canadian manhood" and the "pick of the nation's sinew and brain." Standing in the ranks were men like Corporal William Hart-McHarg, a thirty-year-old law student and crack shot from British Columbia, who had given up his second lieutenant's rank in the Rossland Rifle Company to join A Company under the command of Captain Henry Arnold, a forty-year-old militia officer from the 90th Winnipeg Rifles.

A short distance away in C Company, Joseph Hilliard Rorke (J. Hilliard Rorke, as he liked to style himself) had travelled to Toronto from the Owen Sound area, where he was a journalist. Just a month shy of his twenty-third birthday, and a lieutenant in the 31st Grey Regiment, Rorke joined as a private. Standing with him in C Company's ranks was Private James Findlay, twenty-seven, from the 35th Simcoe

Foresters, another central Ontario militia unit. Nearby, in D Company, Private Richard Rowland Thompson—"Dick," to his friends—shivered in the cold. A blue-eyed, fair-haired man with big ears and a pointed chin, the twenty-two-year-old Irish-born former medical student had served in the 43rd Ottawa and Carleton Rifles.

Standing at the head of the troops was Canada's most experienced soldier, Lieutenant-Colonel William Dillon Otter, fifty-six, chosen by the government to command the new unit. Otter had risen to his position more by longevity than by talent. Although he was a capable enough officer, his austere personality was not the type to inspire men.

Standing behind Otter were his two majors, both regular officers. Lawrence Buchan was a jovial and popular infantry officer, while French-Canadian Oscar Pelletier was an artillery-man and the son of the speaker of the Senate. Buchan also served as Otter's second-in-command.

A captain commanded each of the eight companies, assisted by three lieutenants and a colour sergeant (a sergeant-major in today's terms). The companies were further divided into four sections, each commanded by a sergeant, with a corporal to assist him.

About a hundred and fifty of the officers and men were regulars from Canada's permanent force. Although almost all of the remainder claimed they had served with various militia units across the country, this was not the case. Otter quickly discovered that the majority of them—including officers—knew as little about soldering "as the rawest recruit." In reality only half of the men had prior military service, and many of them had little formal training.

As the rain continued to fall on the parade in Quebec, British Major-General Edward Hutton, the general officer commanding the Canadian militia, inspected the sodden, shivering troops drawn up in long rows in front of him on the Esplanade. When the GOC, as he was usually called, was finished, the governor general, Lord Minto, reviewed the contingent.

Officers of the Royal Canadian Regiment pose with dignitaries at Quebec City before their departure for South Africa in October 1899. Lieutenant-Colonel Otter stands in the centre, helmetless and with a paper protruding from his pocket, flanked by Major Buchan on his right and Major Pelletier on his left. Prime Minister Sir Wilfrid Laurier stands behind and to the left, wearing a top hat.

Speeches came next. The GOC, the governor general, the prime minister, and even Mayor Simon-Napoléon Parent of Quebec stepped to the podium and exhorted the troops in imperial hyperbole typical of the day. Prime Minister Laurier's speech topped them all when he said, "This is a unique occasion in the history of the world."

After what seemed like ages, the formalities and speech-making finally ended. It was none too soon in the soldiers' minds; they had been standing at attention for three hours in the wet and cold, burdened with full packs and equipment weighing thirty-five kilograms. Bill Hart-McHarg, J. Hilliard Rorke, Dick Thompson, Jim Findlay, and their comrades were thankful to be moving again, working out the stiffness in their chilled limbs.

Bands from the city's Royal Canadian Garrison Artillery and Montreal's 5th Royal Scots led the contingent through the streets towards the docks. They marched past throngs of cheering people shouting themselves hoarse and onto their waiting ship, an old Allan Line steamer, the *Sardinian*, a hastily refitted cattle boat. Gaily coloured flags and banners adorned the ship's rigging in an attempt to brighten her normal drab appearance.

One member of the unit was already on the ship, having missed the parade. Private Ted Deslauriers, a twenty-eight-year-old grocery clerk and a corporal in Ottawa's Princess Louise Dragoon Guards, had been carried aboard ill. Deslauriers was well-known to his comrades as a joker and the life of any party, and had been drinking to excess the night before.

The steamship carried 1,039 members of the RCR—twenty of them stowaways who were determined to get into the war—and twenty-two others going to South Africa for various duties, including four nurses, four newspaper correspondents, three chaplains, and a representative from the Young Men's Christian Association.

At 4:30 p.m., the *Sardinian* moved away from the dock and headed down the broad St. Lawrence River. Every vantage point ashore was covered with people. Bill Hart-McHarg, the former lieutenant from British Columbia, was moved by the scene: "The weather-beaten ramparts of the Citadel rising majestically above the surrounding cliffs, re-echoing the cheers of thousands of people, and the accompanying boom of cannon as flags were lowered and the ship moved slowly downstream, left an impression on the mind not easily eradicated."

As the sounds of the Citadel's thirty-two-gun salute faded, small boats laden with more cheering spectators accompanied the ship downstream for the first part of her voyage. Suddenly, the sun burst forth from behind the clouds that had been hiding it for the past few days. Everyone on board took it as a good omen.

The contingent had been so hastily assembled that there was no time for training. Otter hoped the long voyage would provide an opportunity to instruct the soldiers in at least some of the basics of military knowledge, but the cramped conditions aboard the former cattle boat precluded doing much.

In Bill Hart-McHarg's opinion, the ship "was altogether unfitted to convey over a thousand men on such a long voyage, and we could look forward to a period of considerable and quite unnecessary discomfort...it was almost impossible to move about." J. Hilliard Rorke thought there were about "five hundred men too many aboard."

Crowding wasn't the only problem on the tiny ship, which was quickly—and appropriately—nicknamed the "Sardine" by the troops. Despite vast quantities of food, much of it provided by patriotic citizens, meals were a monotonous and overcooked routine of boiled beef, potatoes, and bread. The drinking water was always tepid, and had to be controlled by placing a guard on the tap as there wasn't enough to go around.

The *Sardinian* was propelled by a single screw at an average of under ten knots—about eighteen kilometres per hour. At that rate, it would take a month to steam to South Africa. The ship encountered fine weather for the first few days before a storm struck, giving most aboard their first taste of seasickness. The tiny ship pitched and rolled, incapacitating most of the soldiers. All thoughts of military routine quickly faded.

J. Hilliard Rorke, displaying some of his journalistic bent, recorded the battalion's first fatality in his diary—that of comedian and party-goer Ted Deslauriers: "A peculiar feeling spread through all when it was learned that we had lost the first man of the thousand. Poor fellow died in the hospital in the early morning. Burial at sea at 4:30 p.m. Short Catholic service. Flag removed from corpse. Every hand to cap to salute. Dull, awful splash, then all was over."

Deslauriers' condition worsened after he was brought aboard ill four days earlier, and he had been in intensive care ever since. Although the cause of his death was officially listed as "heart failure," Lieutenant-Colonel Otter as well as Deslauriers' friends thought it was the result of his drinking to excess the night before departure.

Bill Hart-McHarg found that the sanitary and lavatory arrangements were far from adequate; an outbreak of dysentery only added to the soldiers' misery. Once the ship entered warmer climates, there were no awnings to protect the troops and sleeping below decks became nearly impossible. Part of the problem was that no one in authority had any previous experience in organizing a troopship.

Aboard ship, little practical training took place for the job ahead. Instead, Lieutenant-Colonel Otter imposed a daily routine that started at 5 a.m. and was better suited to a peacetime barracks than to a ship taking a unit to war. He was so fussy that the men dubbed him the "Old Woman."

Lieutenant-Colonel Otter insisted that the men salute the officers—a practice usually dispensed with aboard ship. Once they reached the tropics, he foolishly ordered the men to go barefoot on the hot steel deck to toughen their feet. He just as stupidly had them expose their lower legs, arms, necks, chests, and faces to prepare them for the African sun. The result was a lot of painfully sunburned soldiers. After numerous complaints, Otter had to rescind his order about bare feet.

A few days from her destination, the *Sardinian* met a freighter steaming northwards and obtained a copy of a South African newspaper. Unbelievably, the Boers held the upper hand. The simple farmers had bottled up British garrisons at Ladysmith in Natal, and Kimberley and Mafeking in Cape Colony, while British columns were making only slow progress to relieve them.

The men were delighted with the news as it meant they were going to have the chance to fight the Boers. They looked forward to the opportunity to show both the Boers—and the British—the sturdy stuff of which Canadians were made. Every man in Canada's first official overseas contingent intended to make his country proud of him. Would they succeed?

Chapter 2
First Blood

The Boer War was going badly for the British. A string of three humiliating defeats that began on December 10, 1899, stunned the British army and the British public, who were more accustomed to their soldiers triumphing repeatedly over poorly armed natives. The press quickly dubbed the period "Black Week."

The most serious reversal of the three occurred to Lieutenant-General Redvers Buller in mid-month, as he attempted to lift the siege of Ladysmith. Buller lost more than eleven hundred men and twenty artillery pieces.

The army relieved Buller as commander-in-chief, but left him in charge of a large portion of the deployed troops known as the Natal Field Force. Diminutive, one-eyed, sixty-seven-year-old Field Marshal Lord Roberts—known affectionately as "Bobs" by the troops—whose only son had been killed under Buller, came out as the new commander. Major-General Lord Kitchener—tall, heavily built, and much more soldierly-looking—served as his chief of staff.

The day after arriving at Cape Town, the RCR boarded two trains for De Aar, a town eight hundred kilometres "up the line" and closer to the front. Every soldier in the contingent wondered what lay ahead—glory, or death?

The first part of the journey was through an agreeable countryside of farms, gardens, and orchards. But once the trains climbed the escarpment and onto the open country-side of the South African veldt, the scenery changed abruptly. Harsh browns and reds replaced the pleasant greens of the coastal plain; scattered stubby bushes and shrubs superseded abundant plant life.

All along the line, people cheered and waved hand-kerchiefs enthusiastically at the Canadians. The troops responded in kind, until at one station Lieutenant-Colonel Otter informed them that there was to be no more cheering. He reminded them they were soldiers now, and not "damned fools." The rationale behind this order was a mystery to British Columbia's Bill Hart-McHarg, who felt all commanding offi-cers should keep their men shouting for as long as possible.

Two days after leaving Cape Town, De Aar was the first of many shocks that the RCR soldiers received in South Africa. A punishing sand storm greeted them shortly after their arrival. They just had time to pitch a few tents before fine, red, driving sand descended upon them with a force that stung hands, necks, and faces; blew into eyes, ears, and noses; got under clothes and into equipment and permeated food.

The storm compelled them to spend the next twelve hours huddled inside their tents, while outside temperatures climbed to more than 32 degrees Celsius in the shade. Unable to cook meals or perform other duties, the men suffered in silence as the suffocating sand swirled about them. "Give me a Manitoba blizzard any day," Bill Hart-McHarg grumbled, "in preference to a South African sandstorm." Even the stoical Lieutenant-Colonel Otter was affected. "I have never spent such a miserable day in my life," he wrote to his wife.

But spirits were still high. In a letter home, newly-promoted Lance Corporal J. Hilliard Rorke recorded his comrades' feelings: "We all go forward with every confidence of victory and our blows will be strengthened by our love of home. We go to win and live...determined to be victorious."

Four days later, the RCR happily boarded trains for Orange River Station, another 120 kilometres up the line. Contrary to the sandstorm at De Aar—and to the generally held opinion that it rarely rained in South Africa—the men pitched tents in a torrential downpour that drenched everyone. Unable to undress that night because of armed Boers reported nearby, the soldiers shivered in their sodden clothes as the temperature plunged unexpectedly. The Canadians were not used to such sudden extremes of hot and cold or wet and dry.

To their universal disappointment, instead of going into battle, the RCR replaced a British unit, the Gordon Highlanders, in administrative duties at the station. The Canadians grumbled, convinced that the Gordons were marching off to steal their glory.

Two days later, the RCR moved north again, crossing the tawny Orange River and travelling in open railcars for the first time. Unit wags described them as "observation cars—the latest thing in America." The unit traversed a russet-coloured prairie devoid of trees or grass to Belmont, thirty kilometres away and the site of a recent clash between Boers and British. Half-buried bodies of the enemy and bloated horses still littered the blood-red sand of the battle-field, filling the dusty, fly-filled air with a nauseating smell. The grisly sight and foul stench made the Canadians realize that they really were in a war zone.

At Belmont, the Canadians acquired new travelling companions that remained with them throughout their time in South Africa—lice—and became closely acquainted with hordes of sand flies continuously hovering around. The first cases of sickness also appeared, the result of camping on the same ground at Orange River where other units had estab-lished refuse and garbage pits—and latrines.

Major Buchan had temporary command of the RCR, while Lieutenant-Colonel Otter was made responsible for organizing the town's defences. The men were delighted, as they liked "Good Old Larry" much more than they did the aloof Otter, whom they considered far too much of a disciplinarian for their easy-going ways.

Major Buchan trained the unit in the surrounding countryside, putting into practice the lessons the British had learned from previous encounters with the enemy. To prevent officers and non-commissioned officers, such as sergeants, from being picked off by Boer snipers, they now dressed the same as the ordinary soldiers, without visible rank badges, and carried rifles. They also dispersed throughout the ranks, rather than remaining in prominent positions at the head of their men.

The drill of firing volleys while standing shoulder to shoulder, for which the British infantry had been justifiably famous for so long, was abandoned. In its place, soldiers practised moving forward in long lines, well spaced out, or in short rushes from cover to cover. At times, they even crawled forward, a tactic unimaginable by British soldiers until they were forced into it by the accuracy of Boer rifle fire.

There was a rather Spartan celebration of Christmas—another hot, dusty day marked by a small piece of stringy chicken and a bottle of warm beer per man—which provided a short interruption to the Canadians' training. As they trained, occasional raids and patrols into the surrounding countryside provided a brief taste of real war.

One of these was a larger operation that started as the 1800s ended. A mixed force, including the 125 men of J. Hilliard Rorke's C Company, marched west to Sunnyside and Douglas. Rorke described the bustling scene:

> *At 2 p.m. Sunday we were standing at the waggons and a few minutes later amid the shouts of the Kaffir [native] drivers, the hissing and cracking of the long bamboo whips over the backs of the not-too-anxious-to-work mules, the long hurry-scurry flight of the dreamy ostriches who had been taking their noon-day rest under the waggons, the good-byes and light talk of the soldiers, the column moved from camp unto the open veldt [prairie] and away we were for a new field.*

The men on the operation welcomed the new year sitting around a campfire on the dark plains, chatting of earlier New Year's Eves, singing, smoking, and storytelling. Then, after a mug of coffee and a biscuit, J. Hilliard Rorke and his mates rolled into their blankets "for a short, sweet time and returned in spirit to the old Canada." Before they returned to Belmont, the six-day foray captured forty-two Boers and provided a few Canadians with their first taste of combat.

In mid-February, the RCR left Belmont for Graspan, the next station up the line. They left their tents behind, but each man brought an overcoat and a blanket, with a rubber ground sheet for every two. At Graspan, they joined the newly formed British 19th Infantry Brigade under Colonel Horace Smith-Dorrien, which now consisted of the RCR and three other infantry units, all regular British battalions.

Field Marshal Lord Roberts' plan was to head eastwards from Graspan across 130 kilometres of open country to outflank the Boers. His goal was Bloemfontein, the Orange Free State capital. To sustain his force away from the railroad, he loaded his supplies into a vast wagon train pulled by oxen, mules, and horses. Soon, a lengthy procession of thirty-seven thousand men, thirty-six thousand animals, and two thousand wagons snaked its way across the arid countryside.

By the time the RCR reached Graspan, most of Lord Roberts' force had already left. The battalion followed at five the next morning, trailing the long column along with the rest of Colonel Smith-Dorrien's 19th Brigade. Progress was agonizingly slow during the first day on the trek as the temperature soared to 46 degrees Celsius—a scorching, dust-clogged, and utterly exhausting experience.

Along with the heat, thirst was the other curse that afflicted the Canadians throughout their time in South Africa. On long, agonizing marches—and there were plenty of them—men could be driven almost mad with thirst, stumbling forward with swollen tongues, cracked lips, and raw throats. In the absence of potable water, soldiers gulped down whatever water they could find, which often led to enteric fever—as typhoid was then called—and sometimes to death.

On the first day trudging across the arid landscape, fifty-two Canadians dropped out. Some of them actually collapsed in the ranks. Although most caught up later, several were too weak to go any further. The men began to appreciate Otter's attempts to harden them.

In the early afternoon, the troops reached a small, isolated farm known as Ramdam, having covered only twenty-one kilometres. Severely dehydrated, and with their canteens empty, the soldiers crowded round the farm's foul, muddy waterhole, where they quenched their parched throats with its slimy contents and refilled their canteens.

One man, sitting limply at the edge of the water, assured Bill Hart-McHarg that he had just drunk five bottles, and was still thirsty. While animals and men drank the water, others bathed in it. Hart-McHarg noted, "Under ordinary circumstances, a man would not care to wash his hands in [water that was] so uninviting." Many men would soon suffer the results.

While the RCR soldiers slogged along, a Boer raid on the British wagon train resulted in the loss of several days' supplies. Field Marshal Lord Roberts had to halve the already inadequate rations, which usually consisted of canned meat and hardtack, a thick biscuit. It was barely enough to keep the fatigued men going.

General Piet Cronje, the sixty-five-year-old commander of the Boer forces in the Orange Free State, along with five thousand men, five hundred wagons, and several families, had retreated to Paardeberg Drift, or ford, on the Modder River. Cronje and his men prepared defensive positions on the north side of the river's sunken riverbed and along a *donga* (dry watercourse) running into it. Eventually they dug more than six kilometres of trenches.

General Cronje sent the families and the wagons to form a *laager* (defensive encampment of wagons) three kilometres further upriver for safety. From what he had seen of the British actions so far, Cronje had a low opinion of his enemy's fighting ability.

Lord Roberts' entire force now converged on Paardeberg Drift. Early on Sunday morning, February 18, the RCR—now reduced to 872 by illness and exhaustion—crested a low rise and reached the ford. The sound of artillery guns and the distant rattle of rifle fire greeted them, sending the hearts of the inexperienced Canadians racing.

Because Lord Roberts was temporarily ill, Lord Kitchener, his chief of staff, assumed command. Kitchener was impatient for action and decided to assault the Boer position. "It is now seven o'clock," he confidently informed his subordinate commanders. "We shall be in the laager by half past ten."

The RCR consumed a breakfast of biscuit and coffee—reinforced by a rum ration—and moved off to join their brigade. Their first task was to cross the Modder, swollen by recent heavy rains to a depth of a metre and a half and a width of forty-five metres. The normally sluggish river raced by at fifteen kilometres per hour. It was too deep and too swift for dog-tired men to cross easily, especially when weighed down with packs and rifles.

The soldiers in Hart-McHarg's and Rorke's companies crossed first. At one crossing point British military engineers had strung a guide rope across the river, while at the other the men linked arms and crossed four or six at a time, laughing and joking the whole way.

By ten o'clock, after shaking the water out of their boots, the RCR were moving again. Colonel Horace Smith-Dorrien, Otter's immediate commander, ordered him to work his way upriver towards the Boer positions, some five kilometres away.

Although Colonel Smith-Dorrien simply wanted the RCR to guard the terrain between his headquarters on Gun Hill—a feature to the north—and the river, Lieutenant-Colonel Otter believed he was supposed to attack the enemy. Amazingly, no one bothered to tell the men where the Boers were located.

Once across the river, Bill Hart-McHarg thought the panorama before him was not unlike the Canadian prairies:

First Blood

"The Modder River cut its way through the open veldt in a sinuous line, the upper parts of the trees which grew in between its banks just showing nicely above them. There was absolutely no cover for the attacking force."

About fifteen hundred metres from the ford, as the leading companies moved down a ridge onto a plain that inclined slightly towards the river, the Boers opened fire. The Canadians calmly extended the spacing between men to about seven paces and continued their advance. Suddenly, a Boer bullet struck twenty-seven-year-old Private James Findlay, from central Ontario, in the heart. He instantly crumpled to the ground, the RCR's first soldier to die in combat in South Africa.

The Boer's accurate fire forced the Canadians to seek whatever limited shelter was available, while they returned fire against an enemy still hidden along the riverbanks. Soldiers dashed forward in short rushes, until they were obliged to continue by crawling on their bellies. After an hour they could go no farther, and crouched behind rock-hard anthills or lay down in shallow folds in the ground.

The RCR had advanced too far towards the enemy. They were in exposed positions, where any movement drew deadly Boer rifle fire. The day grew hotter. Most soldiers had not eaten a proper meal since the previous afternoon, and had to lie under the blistering sun for five hours, becoming increasingly hungry and thirsty. Swarms of ants and flies added to their discomfort.

A group of Boers pose wearing full bandoliers and carrying their high-powered Mauser rifles. These rough farmers turned out to be superior irregular soldiers who outfought the British army on several occasions.

In the early afternoon, an icy rainstorm soaked the men. Although its wonderful coolness provided a brief, delicious relief, it soon left them cold and shivering. As the soldiers tried to shelter from the Boer fire, ammunition-carriers, stretcher-bearers, and runners carrying messages moved about the battlefield. Several were wounded as they carried out their important tasks.

Captain Henry Arnold was shot in the head when he looked up to survey the enemy's position through his binoculars. Three stretcher-bearers in succession were wounded as they tried to get to him. Finally, the junior of the unit's two doctors ran forward, bandaged Arnold's wound, and carried him from the battlefield. Arnold died five days later.

The RCR was not alone in making little progress. None of the British infantry units succeeded in breaking through. A stalemate had developed, with neither side able to get the upper hand. All the British had to do was wait the Boer leader General Piet Cronje out, but Lord Kitchener was impatient for results.

As Kitchener grew more and more frustrated, he galloped from unit to unit, encouraging them to renew their assaults. During one such foray, he discovered a few hundred soldiers from a British unit, the Duke of Cornwall's Light Infantry, sitting idle in the rear. He immediately ordered their commanding officer, Lieutenant-Colonel William Aldworth, to assist the Canadians.

Lieutenant-Colonel Aldworth took his men, crossed the Modder, and headed towards the RCR firing line. At about four in the afternoon, an agitated Aldworth encountered Lieutenant-Colonel Otter and curtly informed the Canadian commander that "he had been sent to finish this business" and "proposed doing so with the bayonet." His tone and manner implied that the RCR had done several things wrong, which resulted in their failure to capture the objective. The cautious Otter pointed out that the distance was too great to charge the Boers, who knew the exact range to every part of the battlefield. Aldworth snapped, "The Cornwalls will show you," and departed.

At 5:15 p.m., Lieutenant-Colonel Aldworth ordered a charge. Bugles sounded and most of the Canadians, frustrated at laying out in the open all day, joined in the British unit's suicidal dash across 550 metres of open ground towards the Boer lines. More than a thousand men charged the enemy positions that day—a dismounted equivalent of the Crimean War's disastrous charge of the Light Brigade.

Attackers fell as a heavy Boer fusillade tore through their ranks. The frenzied assault ground to a halt about halfway to the enemy, unable to go any further. Both Lieutenant-Colonel Aldworth and his adjutant were killed, along with several others. Bill Hart-McHarg called it costly work, but found it "exciting to a degree."

A bugle sounded the recall, but few were able to respond. Now more exposed than ever, the best they could do was hug the ground and wait for darkness. The wounded and dying suffered the worst of all; the memory of their groans and cries for help was something that most survivors never forgot.

Stretcher-bearers and others tried to help the wounded. Dick Thompson ran to the aid of his friend James Bradshaw, who had been shot in the throat. The Ottawa medical student lay beside his comrade, pressing his fingers against Bradshaw's jugular vein to keep him from bleeding to death. Seven hours later Bradshaw was carried to safety under cover of darkness.

First Blood

In a letter to his father in Ireland, Thompson noted, "The air was simply alive with bullets. Every second I could hear the hiss of the Mauser bullet or the short crack of the explosive bullet, as it swished by my head...It was marvellous how I escaped, as my helmet was shot off my head by the Boers."

Thompson later received a thank-you letter from Bradshaw, "My heart's all gone wrong and also my eyesight. Had it not been for you...I would have been a beautiful corpse long ere this, and I really don't know how to thank you sufficiently. Words seem so cold and barren."

Lieutenant-Colonel Otter ordered his men back to Paardeberg Drift for the night, where they rested and ate an inadequate meal of tea and biscuit. At the same time, the Boers withdrew upriver to their main laager, or defensive position, where their families and wagons had already taken shelter. There, they prepared to make a stand, from trenches and dugouts along both sides of the Modder River.

It had not been a good day for the RCR. The desperate fight that marked Canada's first overseas battle had ended in failure. Eighteen Canadians had been killed, three died later from their wounds (including Captain Arnold), and another sixty were wounded. "Bloody Sunday," as the soldiers called it, was the costliest battle for Canada since the War of 1812 and would prove to be the unit's worst day in South Africa.

Chapter 3
Canada's Victory

Lieutenant-Colonel Otter and his men were disheartened by their failure and the loss of so many friends on Bloody Sunday with nothing to show for it. Yet Otter must bear at least some of the blame for the tragedy. When British Lieutenant-Colonel Aldworth told him that he was ordering a charge, Otter, although he did not direct his men to participate in it, did not prevent them from taking part, either. Even as his men moved forward, he did nothing to stop them, nor did he later chastise them.

The main question in the Canadian soldiers' minds was how they had acquitted themselves during their baptism of fire. Bill Hart-McHarg knew that no man had flinched, but he and his comrades wondered what the generals would think. They didn't have long to wait for an answer.

The next morning, the Canadians returned to the battlefield to collect and bury their dead. That afternoon, Colonel Horace Smith-Dorrien visited them. He praised their steadiness during their first experience under fire, hoping to restore their morale. Then he ordered them to occupy an outpost line along the base of Gun Hill, about nine hundred metres from the main Boer defensive position.

The next day was an exasperating repeat of Bloody Sunday. The RCR lay in the open for twelve hours, subjected to scorching sun, hunger, thirst, ants, and flies—all the time under heavy Boer fire.

Over the next few days, under blazing sun and pounding rain, the RCR performed various perimeter duties designed to keep the Boers from escaping. The work was performed "under very disagreeable circumstances," according to Bill Hart-McHarg. "The rain came down in torrents. We were without greatcoats, and had very little to eat." In addition, a mix-up resulted in less than one blanket per man.

Winnipeg's Captain Henry Arnold was buried on the south side of the Modder. His men went down to the gravesite to pay their respects to an officer Hart-McHarg described as "enthusiastic, painstaking, and competent... [who] had endeared himself to every one of his men by the careful manner in which he looked after their interests."

As the British gradually tightened a noose around the Boers, artillery guns shelled the Boers continuously during daylight. Conditions were deplorable inside the Boers' defensive position, which stretched in a three-kilometre arc along the north side of the Modder. The shelling set wagons afire and killed hundreds of animals, while forty-one hundred Boer men, women, and children cowered in the stifling safety of their trenches and dugouts. They came out only at night to dump the carcasses of their dead animals into the Modder, which carried them downstream towards Paardeberg Drift.

Soldiers of the Royal Canadian Regiment cross the Modder River at Paardeberg Drift, using a guide rope set up by British Royal Engineers, on "Bloody Sunday," February 18, 1900. A British artillery unit has crossed just before them.

The Canadians were in pretty bad shape as well. Sickness, injury, and death had reduced the original 1,039 soldiers to 708. Those who remained were a bedraggled lot. Unable to wash or shave most of the time, they wore the same lice-infested clothes they had left Belmont in two weeks earlier. Extremes of heat and cold, as well as insufficient rations, only added to their misery. When the Canadians got the odd rest day at the ford, they washed their bodies and clothes with river water, which they also used for drinking and cooking.

To make matters worse, hundreds of dead animals from the Boer encampment floated downstream, past Paardeberg Drift. Their decomposing bodies polluted the water and filled the air with a sickening stench.

Enteric fever struck again, prompting many to complain that they didn't come to Africa to die of disease for Queen and Country. They came to fight; and if they were to die, then let it be a soldier's death—in battle.

On February 26, the RCR relieved a British unit, the Duke of Cornwall's Light Infantry, in the front trenches opposite the west end of the Boer position, only 550 metres from the dug-in Boers. The next day held a special significance for both sides. Nineteen years earlier, on February 27, 1881, the Boers had triumphed over the British at the Battle of Majuba. The Boers' victory had secured their independence and humiliated the British. Ever since, the British army had been anxious to avenge the defeat.

The responsibility for the attack fell to Colonel Smith-Dorrien's 19th Brigade, which had been reinforced by additional infantry units and Royal Engineers. Because the RCR manned the front line trenches, they would lead the assault, assisted by the British. Lieutenant-Colonel Otter received his orders at about three in the afternoon of February 26. The raw Canadians were about to undertake one of the most difficult operations in warfare—a night attack.

By 10 p.m., the forward RCR companies (C through H)—now reduced by illness, injury, and death from their original 125 men each—were in position for the assault. Their trenches stretched northwards for more than three hundred metres from the riverbank. A and B companies, which lost the most men on Bloody Sunday, were given other tasks. Bill Hart-McHarg's A Company was sent south of the river, while B Company was held in reserve.

Shortly after two in the dark morning of February 27, five hundred Canadians climbed out of their trenches as quietly as possible and formed two lines six paces apart. The front line had bayonets fixed. To keep direction in the darkness, the soldiers advanced shoulder-to-shoulder, "clasping the hands of those on our left," according to J. Hilliard Rorke.

Bill Hart-McHarg described the scene:

> *Slowly feeling their way in the darkness over*
> *the uneven and broken ground, the men in*

*the two lines moved forward. Not a word
was spoken, and every possible precaution
was taken against any noise being made.
One hundred! two hundred! three hundred
yards! The tension was getting extreme.
They knew they were advancing on a
perfectly constructed trench, held by resolute
and desperate men, each armed with the
quick-firing Mauser. Eyes tried to pierce the
darkness, but nothing could be seen. Were
the Boers by any chance asleep? Would they
be able to reach those trenches and decide
the question solely with the cold steel? Four
hundred yards! The men were breathing
hard, not from exertion, but from nervous
excitement. They were surely within striking
distance now, whatever happened. Despite
the darkness and the unknown ground a few
more yards gained would surely enable them
to rush those trenches and use the bayonet.*

Then, around a quarter to three, when the Canadians
were less than a hundred metres from the enemy trenches, a
soldier bumped into a tin can filled with rocks hanging from
a wire. The primitive warning system alerted Boer sentries,
and their first shots rang out.

A withering fire quickly followed from the Boer lines as the defenders scrambled out of their dugouts. Fortunately, the sentries' shots gave the Canadians enough time to throw themselves to the ground and avoid the worst of it. British Royal Engineers started to dig in while the Canadians returned fire.

Although the casualties from the first shots were surprisingly light, the soldiers who were closest to the Boer lines—in some cases only sixty metres—suffered the most. This was a group of Maritimers, who suffered eight killed and nineteen wounded in the opening volley.

For the next fifteen minutes, the two sides traded shots. The RCR front line kept up a steady fire, while the second line and the engineers dug in. A few soldiers, paralysed by fear, hugged the ground and didn't fire at anything.

Suddenly, an authoritative voice from the left flank called out, "Retire and bring back your wounded!" Most of the soldiers were only too happy to oblige. The Canadian fire lessened, men stood up and ran to the rear. As they fled, fire from the Boers felled several.

Soldiers of four companies (C, D, E, and F) were soon crammed into their original trenches, now occupied by the Gordon Highlanders. They remained there for the rest of the battle. But the two companies from the Maritimes (G and H, under Lieutenant Archie Macdonnell and Captain Duncan Stairs respectively) either did not hear the order or purposely chose to ignore it and stood their ground, along with some Royal Engineers.

Dawn revealed several bodies lying on the battlefield. Dick Thompson, who had saved James Bradshaw on Bloody Sunday, described what happened when one of the casualties appeared to move: "I jumped over the trenches and ran straight for the Boer position in broad daylight, and under a heavy fire, to bring in a wounded comrade. I had to go about three hundred yards to get him but the poor fellow just died after I reached him."

A British soldier who witnessed Thompson's actions noted, "Although the bullets whistled around him, he coolly regained his trenches with a pipe stuck between his teeth. I have never, during the campaign, seen a case of such courage and pluck as that displayed by Private Thompson."

Thompson quickly repeated his earlier feat and went to the aid of another soldier. His immediate commander and Lieutenant-Colonel Otter both recommended Thompson for the Victoria Cross—the highest decoration possible—for his actions that day and on the eighteenth. Although he did not receive the medal, he was given an award that was even rarer.

Queen Victoria followed the fortunes of her soldiers in the field with interest. For the first Christmas of the war, in 1899, she sent each of her "dear brave soldiers" in South Africa a tin box of chocolate, bearing her portrait and bound with red, white, and blue ribbon. They became highly prized souvenirs. J. Hilliard Rorke sent his home to his mother.

When the elderly Queen learned that the high South African plains could be bitterly cold at night, she personally crocheted eight khaki-coloured scarves, each bearing her royal cipher "VRI" stitched in white cotton in a corner. Half were to be given to British soldiers and the others to the "four most distinguished private soldiers in the Colonial Forces of Canada, Australia, New Zealand and Cape Colony." Lieutenant-Colonel Otter and his men nominated Thompson for the Queen's Scarf, which he later received.

At first light, from the safety of their hastily-dug new trenches, the 120 Maritimers, who had not withdrawn, realized that they were overlooking the enemy. They could fire into the main Boer position, as well as into Boer dugouts in the riverbank.

When darkness began to fade around four o'clock, several Boers emerged from their trenches to survey the battlefield. The Maritimers immediately opened up with well-disciplined fire that drove the enemy back into their holes in the ground. The Boers returned fire for about an hour or so, then those in the forward enemy trenches shouted that they wanted to surrender.

Initially, the Canadians continued to fire on the Boers. They had heard several stories about Boers pretending to give up, only to open fire again. Around six o'clock, a lone Boer climbed out of his trench carrying a white flag and walked towards the Canadians. All firing ceased immediately. Other Boers quickly followed, surrendering to the Canadian soldiers.

The Boer capitulation cheered Lieutenant-Colonel Otter's spirits, as much as he had been disheartened by the sight of his men breaking and running during the night. The victory of the soldiers from the Maritimes now overshadowed that earlier disgrace, and the matter was quietly dropped. It was never ascertained who had given the order to retire.

The leading British and Canadian troops advanced warily, bayonets fixed, past the Boer trenches and into the main position. They never forgot the sight that greeted them.

For days, over a hundred artillery guns had pounded the position, reducing the Boer wagons and carts to burned-out skeletons. The putrid carcasses of dead animals that had not been dumped into the river littered the ground, along with debris of all kinds: artillery ammunition, trunks, mattresses, saddles, harnesses, household furniture, children's clothing. Gradually the rest of the Boers emerged from their trenches and holes. Bill Hart-McHarg noted they were a motley crew of all ages, clinging to whatever seemed precious at the time: blankets, pots and pans, articles of food.

Hart-McHarg was astonished that this ragged, grubby, dishevelled lot had held them off for nine days and inflicted heavy casualties. The thought uppermost in his mind was "what a power the modern rifle is in the hands of a man who knows how to use it, acting on the defensive." Surprisingly, there were only about three hundred casualties among the forty-one hundred Boers left in the position. Deep trenches and dugouts had saved lives.

The British commander, Field Marshal Lord Roberts, arrived to accept the surrender of the Boers from their commander, General Piet Cronje. A correspondent from the London *Times* described the old Boer leader's "great square shoulders from which the heavy beard was thrown forward so that he seemed humped; a heavy face, shapeless with unkempt, grey-tipped black hair; lowering under heavy brows, from which small, cunning, foxy eyes peered shiftily."

General Cronje rode a small, grey pony, and was wearing a wide-brimmed hat, a short overcoat, and tweed trousers. His face was deeply burned from the sun. After breakfast with Lord Roberts, the old man and his wife were sent into exile on St. Helena, the same South Atlantic island to which the British had banished Napoleon Bonaparte after his final defeat at Waterloo in 1815.

Most Boers never forgave General Cronje for surrendering, especially on the anniversary of their great victory at Majuba. Although Cronje was a resolute and brave leader, he did not have the intelligence, flexibility, and drive necessary to be a successful general. His decision to dig in at Paardeberg Drift gave away the Boers' greatest asset—their mobility—and was a crucial blunder. Cronje's untimely and unexpected capitulation—with nearly ten per cent of the entire Boer army—opened the way to Bloemfontein for the British.

Late that afternoon, as the RCR searched the Boer position for souvenirs and food—an honour they were given in recognition of their role in the victory—Lord Roberts rode over to congratulate the Canadians. He praised them and acknowledged them as being "instrumental in the capture of General Cronje and his forces." "'Canadian,'" he went on to state, "now stands for bravery, dash, and courage." J. Hilliard Rorke noted the other units had dubbed the Canadians "the fire-eaters."

Colonel Smith-Dorrien, Lieutenant-Colonel Otter, and the army echoed their commander's accolades. Once Lord Roberts' dispatches reached Britain, Canada and the rest of the Empire heaped praise upon the soldiers of the RCR. Canadian soldiers had just won their first foreign victory, and it was the first significant British success of the war. It quickly became known as "The Dawn of Majuba Day," avenging the stain of the earlier defeat. Many hailed it as a turning point in the conflict and the beginning of the reversal of British fortunes. At a cost of thirteen dead and thirty wounded, the RCR had earned Canada's first foreign battle honour: Paardeberg.

Lieutenant-Colonel Otter was restrained, rather than enthusiastic. "Yes, we avenged Majuba," he wrote to a cousin, "and a damned nasty job we had of it—not many are likely to forget that morning during the remainder of our natural lives."

That night, J. Hilliard Rorke wrote to his mother from the former Boer camp. Despite the victory, he reflected on the general pessimism—and his own determination: "This field life is hard. Never under canvas, never sure of meals, either a feast or famine—generally a famine, long tramps and heavy duties. The majority of the boys are getting pretty tired of it, but I know it is what we enlisted to do and I am going to do it."

Chapter 4
Adventures on Horseback

Two days after the Royal Canadian Regiment left Quebec City to fight the Boers in far-off South Africa, the Canadian government offered another contingent to the British, who turned down the proposal, still supremely confident in the ability of their army to overcome a rabble of ignorant farmers. The three disastrous defeats of the Black Week of December 1899 abruptly changed that opinion and the British accepted the Canadians' offer.

By now, the British realized that mounted troops were much better than foot soldiers for the type of war being waged in South Africa, and this time requested cavalry and artillery.

Canada complied by raising two mounted units, each of two squadrons (the cavalry equivalent of infantry companies), and an artillery unit of three batteries (the artillery equivalent of infantry companies).

One mounted unit was based on the country's only permanent force cavalry unit, the Royal Canadian Dragoons (RCD), augmented by militiamen and volunteers from eastern Canada and Manitoba. The other was based on the North West Mounted Police (NWMP) and brought up to strength by men from the Northwest Territories, many of them former Mounties. The artillery unit came from the militia, built around a core of permanent force gunners.

The two mounted units were designated the 1st and 2nd Battalions, Canadian Mounted Rifles; at 371 all ranks, they were smaller than infantry units. Majors commanded each of the units' two squadrons, which were further divided into four troops (the cavalry equivalent of infantry platoons) of about forty men under lieutenants. Both battalions had two horse-drawn Maxim or Colt machine guns, mounted on light galloping carriages.

Lieutenant-Colonel François Lessard, thirty-nine, commanding officer of the RCD, was in charge of 1 CMR, while Lieutenant-Colonel Lawrence Herchmer, fifty-nine, the NWMP commissioner, commanded 2 CMR. Two experienced officers acted as their deputies. Lieutenant-Colonel Thomas Evans, who had commanded B Squadron of the

RCD, became Lessard's second-in-command with the rank of major. Herchmer's deputy was Sam Steele, who soon went off to form another unit, Strathcona's Horse.

Lieutenant-Colonel Charles Drury, forty, another permanent force officer, commanded the 539-man artillery unit. Each of its three batteries (C, D, and E) was commanded by a major and had six 12-pounder breech-loading guns, which could fire up to 4,700 metres. Each battery was further broken down into three sections (the artillery equivalent of infantry platoons) of two guns each, commanded by lieutenants.

Rather than the permanent force rates of pay that the RCR received, remuneration for all mounted units was at the NWMP rate—from 75¢ a day for a private up to $7.12 for a lieutenant-colonel. The RCR soldiers complained vociferously, to no avail.

The RCD, originally formed in 1883, were proud of their cavalry roots and objected to being categorized as mounted infantry, so Lessard led a concerted campaign to restore their original name. Ultimately, he was successful, and the Dragoons received permission to use their original title a few months after they arrived in South Africa, at which time 2 CMR officially became 1 CMR, although it was usually known simply as "the CMR." These name changes did not take effect until August 1900, but the titles RCD and CMR will be used from this point on to avoid confusion.

In Halifax, the Dragoons had rejected William Anderson of Saint John, New Brunswick, because he failed his riding test. Still determined to join, he hung around the barracks, learned to ride on his own, and stowed away aboard the ship that carried the regiment to South Africa.

Hidden away in the depths of the *Milwaukee*, Anderson suffered solitary bouts of seasickness and was sustained by food from friends. He came out of hiding only after the ship was well out to sea. When an officer noticed him, he was charged with being aboard illegally. Anderson's "punishment" was just what he wanted—he was immediately sworn in!

Although most of the men suffered from seasickness, the horses had it far worse. Crammed into narrow stalls on the lower decks, they were at the mercy of the waves. A violent lurch could send a horse crashing to the deck and it took several men to get a downed beast on its feet again. Icy seawater ran down to the lower decks and remained until the scuppers—clogged with sawdust and dung—were cleared. Meanwhile, the horses had to stand in the chilly water.

The soldiers recovered from seasickness, but many horses did not. In their cold and weakened state, several caught pneumonia. Their heads drooped and discharge dripped from their noses as they leaned against their stalls and refused to eat. The troopers did everything they could to help. They tempted them with gruel, rubbed their legs, treated their cuts and sores, comforted them—and even poured good army rum down their throats.

Despite the soldiers' best efforts, several horses died on each ship en route to South Africa, but a board of officers had to formally approve the write-off of every dead animal before its carcass could be thrown overboard to the sharks. Although the regulation was probably designed to prevent the soldiers from selling horses, at sea it seemed the height of bureaucratic madness to these soldiers.

Compared to the Canadian infantry and the artillery— who essentially wore the same uniforms as British soldiers—the appearance of the mounted troops caused great excitement in Cape Town when they arrived in March 1900. To the townsfolk, these big, brawny Canadians riding their huge horses on high-horned heavy western stock saddles were something out of the fabled Wild West with their cowboy hats, high boots, spurs, and Colt revolvers.

The mounted Canadians were a tough, hard-riding lot, and some of their exploits quickly became the stuff of legend. For example, CMR Corporal Joseph Clarkson of Brandon, Manitoba, was always given the hardest scouting tasks because he could get the job done and always be depended upon to do a little bit extra.

On one occasion, the CMR was told to send a patrol into Vredefort, a small town along a rail line, to find out if Boers occupied it. Within two kilometres of the town, Clarkson and his six horsemen surprised a Boer outpost. Clarkson demanded their surrender, claiming in a loud voice to be a British general. The Boers handed over their rifles and were sent away on foot, while the troopers took their horses to replace their own weary mounts.

Leaving two men to guard captured Boer equipment and supplies, Clarkson led the three remaining horsemen into Vredefort without meeting any opposition. He rode up to the mayor's office and loudly demanded the town's surrender, claiming to be the British commander-in-chief. He then ordered the townsfolk to deliver all arms and ammunition to the market square, collecting about fifty rifles in the process, which he sent back to the British in a wagon.

Then Clarkson took down the Boer flag and ran up the Union Jack. To add insult to injury, he even had his picture taken standing in the middle of a group of Boers. Corporal Clarkson is smiling broadly, but one hand is firmly on the butt of his Colt revolver.

The CMR and the artillery (except for one of its three batteries—a third of the unit) received orders to join an ad hoc unit called the Carnarvon Field Force, under Colonel Sir Charles Parsons. Parsons' task was to pacify some two or three thousand rebellious Boer settlers in the north-central part of Cape Colony, a region known as the Great Karroo.

Lieutenant Edward "Dinky" Morrison, one of the Canadian artillery officers, described the Karroo as "a most God-forsaken region—a stony plain, with here and there hills of khaki dust, their faces pock-marked with bunches of blue-green sage brush."

By mid-March, the Canadian units were encamped along the rail line 650 kilometres northeast of Cape Town. Besides the CMR and the Canadian artillery, the Carnarvon Field Force consisted of three mounted companies from Britain, Australia, and New Zealand. A wagon train with supplies for seven days brought up the rear of the column.

A four-day march to the northwest brought the troops to Carnarvon, about a hundred and thirty kilometres from the railway, on St. Patrick's Day. For the Canadians, it had been a tough introduction to the South African climate and terrain. Plagued by a shortage of water and a blinding sandstorm, the force creaked across the arid countryside at the pace of the slowest oxen and mules.

A sudden, violent sandstorm struck the column's camp at Carnarvon. It bowled tents over, blew their contents about, and covered meals with a fine layer of sand, causing the men's spoons to rasp on their plates as they ate their dinner.

Colonel Parsons' Carnarvon Field Force set off again the next day, headed towards Van Wyks Vlei. It was tough going in the treeless, near-desert of the Karroo, which had been experiencing a drought for two years. The column moved from one watering place to another, carrying all its needs, including forage for the animals. Nevertheless, many of the horses simply gave out and died.

Lieutenant Morrison quickly realized the importance of water in South Africa: "It will give you some idea of the way good water is valued in this country to explain that if a man is giving you a drink he hands over the bottle of whiskey and makes you say 'when' to the pouring of the water."

At Van Wyks Vlei, a sudden downpour ended the lengthy drought and washed out sections of the main road. The supply wagons couldn't get through, forcing man and beast to go on half rations for ten days. When the rain ended four days later, the previously parched earth was a sticky, muddy morass.

Leaving the main body at Van Wyks Vlei, Colonel Parsons led an advance guard to Kenhardt, sending ahead some mounted soldiers under Captain Archie Macdonnell and two artillery guns under Lieutenant John McCrae. Macdonnell went on to command 1st Canadian Division during the last eighteen months of World War I, while McCrae served as a doctor in that same war and wrote perhaps the most famous of all war poems—"In Flanders Fields."

By the time the Canadians struggled through the clinging mud to Kenhardt, the Boers had fled, leaving twelve whites and five hundred natives behind. When Colonel Parsons arrived, he reclaimed the town for Britain. The troops stayed in the depressing little town for five days, many of them sick with dysentery.

With nothing to do, several CMR soldiers went on a binge that resulted in nineteen of them being thrown into the

Soldiers of the Royal Canadian Regiment enjoy an all-too-rare chance to have a bath in South Africa, 1900, where it was said that water was scarcer than whiskey.

local jail. When the British threatened to send them home, Captain Macdonnell managed to appease the authorities and convince his men that any such future behaviour would quickly end their soldiering days.

By mid-April, the Carnarvon Field Force was finished in De Aar. Its mission accomplished, it was broken up and its units dispersed. The Canadian artillery was left to help guard stations along the rail line between De Aar and Belmont, while the CMR was sent to Bloemfontein.

The first real experience of Canadian mounted troopers and gunners in the war had been less than satisfying. Many of them would remember it as their hardest time in South Africa. The long ride had been plagued by extremes of weather, sickness, and boredom. Even worse, the Canadians did not fight any Boers, which, after all, was the reason they had come to this far-off land.

Chapter 5
The Queen's Cowboys

[handwritten: Baron Strathcona = Donald Alexander Smith]

Donald Alexander Smith emigrated to Canada from his native Scotland as an eighteen-year-old in 1838, the same year that Queen Victoria was crowned. Through family contacts, Smith obtained employment with the Hudson's Bay Company as an apprentice at the very bottom of the organization. Over the next fifty years, he rose steadily until he reached the top position, governor, in 1889.

Donald Smith amassed a sizeable fortune and moved into public life. He was knighted in 1886; appointed Canadian high commissioner in London, England, in 1896; and elevated to the peerage as the first Baron Strathcona and Mount

Royal the next year. Lord Strathcona was very much a man of his times: a loyal, patriotic Canadian and a supporter of a strong, united British Empire.

When the war broke out in South Africa, Lord Strathcona quickly realized that the type of men he had encountered on the Canadian prairies—men used to living and fighting from the saddle, like Mounties and cowboys—would be of far greater use than meticulously drilled infantrymen.

Lord Strathcona wired Canadian Prime Minister Sir Wilfrid Laurier, stating:

> *Should like to provide and send to South*
> *Africa my personal fund squadron mounted*
> *men and officers say four hundred men*
> *and horses from North West...Men must be*
> *expert marksmen, at home in saddle, and*
> *efficient as rough riders and rangers.*

Prime Minister Laurier quickly accepted the generous offer. Lord Strathcona immediately set aside £150,000 in the Bank of Montreal (of which he was president) to cover the costs of raising the new unit. On the unit's arrival in South Africa, the British government would be responsible for it, and for its return to Canada.

Consideration of who should raise and command the unit resulted in the inspired choice of renowned NWMP

Superintendent Samuel Benfield Steele. Sam Steele, forty-nine, was a six-foot, barrel-chested man of exceptional endurance and strength; on a dare, he once lifted a 136-kilogram load on his shoulders and walked with it. Superintendent Steele was known throughout the West. He had served in the militia during the Fenian Raids of 1866, participated in the Red River Expedition of 1870, joined the permanent force artillery in 1871, and transferred to the NWMP when it was formed in 1873.

Sam Steele was commissioned in 1878, took part in the Northwest Rebellion, and fought in the last battle on Canadian soil at Steele's Narrows in 1885. During the Klondike Gold Rush of 1898, he was in charge of the Mounties in the Yukon.

Given the rank of lieutenant-colonel to command the new unit, Sam Steele had carte blanche to select the best riders and marksmen in the West. By now, the size of the unit had been increased to five hundred men, divided into three squadrons. One squadron would come from each of Manitoba, the Northwest Territories (today's Saskatchewan and Alberta), and British Columbia.

Sam Steele noted the majority of the men were "the very pick of the cowboy, cowpuncher, policeman, and ex-policeman...The balance are Westerners of varied experiences, especially qualified with rifle and horse...all of them used to long hours in the saddle, experienced men...and well used to hard work, range riding, patrolling, surveying, prospecting, freighting and farming." They were exactly the type of hardy individual the British so desperately needed in South Africa.

The response across the West was overwhelming and in two weeks Lieutenant-Colonel Steele signed up enough men and officers for the unit, to be known as Strathcona's Horse. Many more had to be turned down, including six hundred Arizona cowboys who volunteered to bring their own horses and rifles. Men from each locality were kept together, under an officer from the same area whenever possible.

There were some oddities among the adventurers. Edward Seymour was the drunken son of the Marquis of Hereford. James Pinder inherited £100,000 just after he signed up; he was granted a month's leave to put his affairs in order. "Old George" Gamsby always managed to be absent whenever a group photograph was being taken; apparently American law officers were on the lookout for him. John Brothers had gone into the Klondike during the gold rush and come out a wealthy man.

Others had military or Mountie experience. Captain Edward Parker, a crack shot and expert horseman, had been forced to resign his British army commission in the Essex Regiment for "conduct unbecoming an officer" and settled in British Columbia. He reverted to the rank of sergeant so he could join the new unit, bringing a group of men from Cranbrook and Fort Steele with him. Lieutenant-Colonel

Steele made Parker's friend, ex-NWMP Inspector M. H. White-Fraser, their lieutenant.

Corporal Arthur Richardson, nicknamed "Tappy," had emigrated from England when he was nineteen and joined the NWMP in 1894. He was serving at Battleford when he joined Strathcona's Horse, and was made a sergeant.

By the military standards of the day, Strathcona's Horse was an unconventional body of men. The governor-general, Lord Minto, more used to parade-ground peacocks, praised them in public, but described them as "useless ruffians, the lame, the halt and blind" in private. Time would soon tell who was the better judge of men—a pampered English earl or a rough-and-ready Canadian Mountie.

The men travelled to Ottawa, where the unit was formed. They had signed on for a minimum of six months and a maximum of one year. For their service, privates would receive 75¢ per day, corporals 85¢, sergeants $1, and sergeants-major $1.50.

In Ottawa, the men were accommodated in cattle sheds at Lansdowne Park exhibition grounds and bedded down on straw mattresses. They were issued weapons—.303 Lee Enfield rifles and .45 Colt revolvers. Each trooper received two blue serge uniforms with white collars and red piping, two khaki duck uniforms, a "wedgie" field cap, a wide-brimmed Stetson, a toque, two pairs of ankle boots, two pairs of riding boots, and an overcoat.

Fifteen-year old Edwin "Mickey" McCormick made his way to Ottawa from his Toronto home, hoping to join Strathcona's Horse, the new unit he had heard about. McCormick had even written to the unit's commanding officer, the legendary Sam Steele, claiming to be sixteen, a qualified trumpeter, and an experienced rider. He was none of these.

In Ottawa, the regimental sergeant-major paraded McCormick before the commanding officer, who sternly demanded a militia trumpeter's certificate and a letter from his mother. It was obvious Lieutenant-Colonel Steele knew the boy had none of these—and was underage as well. As the sergeant-major started to march the teenager out, Steele called to him, "Just a minute, McCormick. Your mother wrote to me and I know she really doesn't want you to come, but you'd leave home anyway. So I'll have to be a father to you as well as your colonel and keep you out of trouble."

To keep an eye on Mickey McCormick, Lieutenant-Colonel Steele appointed him as his trumpeter and orderly. Undoubtedly Steele recalled the day thirty-six years earlier, when he himself had claimed he was sixteen, so he could join the army.

On St. Patrick's Day, 1900, Strathcona's Horse sailed from Halifax on the *Monterey*. The long voyage was marred by the loss of 176 horses at sea to pneumonia. One day, as another dead horse was thrown overboard to waiting sharks, a trooper

Soldiers of Strathcona's Horse are pictured aboard the SS Monterey, *en route to South Africa, March–April 1900.*

was heard to remark, "I guess we'll be Strathcona's Foot by the time we get to South Africa." On arrival in Cape Town on April 10, 1900, another forty-four animals were suffering from glanders, an infectious, often fatal disease, and had to be put down. It was a bad start for a unit that depended on horses.

After replacing their lost mounts, Strathcona's Horse entered enemy territory on June 20, when they reached Zand Spruit to reinforce Lieutenant-General Redvers Buller as he resumed his advance on Johannesburg. Buller, who had spent seven years in Canada with his unit and had taken part in the Red River Expedition of 1870, was impressed by the physique of the men of Strathcona's Horse. Buller—himself a large man noted for his strength—asked Lieutenant-Colonel Steele, "Why did you bring such big men as mounted troops?" "Well, sir," Steele replied, "I looked all over Canada and these were the smallest men I could find." Buller burst out laughing. "I am something of a liar myself," he declared, "but you beat me."

By this stage of the war, Lieutenant-General Buller's shortcomings were painfully obvious to everyone. Although he was adored by the troops and his personal bravery was never in question—he had earned the Victoria Cross during the Zulu War of 1879—he was not a good senior commander. Buller was indecisive, procrastinating, and ineffectual. Worse, he had suffered a string of defeats, resulting in the nickname "Sir Reverse Buller." Many wondered why he had not been removed from command.

Within Buller's command, known as the Natal Field Force, Strathcona's Horse was assigned to the 3rd Mounted Brigade. Two days after Strathcona's Horse arrived, Buller's force reached Standerton in the Transvaal and received a warm welcome from the town's British citizens. The Strathcona's remained there until the end of June, when they began to move west along the railway.

In the weeks following Dominion Day, Strathcona's Horse fought a guerrilla campaign against the Boers, who called them the "Big Stirrups" because of the large wooden stirrups on their western saddles. At any given time, one detachment of soldiers or another was always in close proximity to the Boers, acting as scouts or flank guards.

In early July a reinforcement draft, consisting of one lieutenant and fifty troopers for the Strathcona's, reached Standerton. While they awaited orders, the new troopers took part in several patrols and received their baptism of fire before they even reached the unit.

On July 5, at Wolve Spruit, some twenty-five kilometres north of Standerton, thirty-eight Strathcona's encountered a force of about eighty Boers. The two sides quickly engaged at short range until the Canadians were ordered to retire. As they wheeled around and galloped back, Private Alex McArthur was injured in the arm and leg when his horse stumbled and fell on him.

Sergeant Tappy Richardson was one of those who had been sent to bring the reinforcements forward. When he saw the difficulty Private McArthur was in, he rode back several hundred metres to help him. He pulled the wounded man from under the horse, threw him over his saddle, and desperately galloped off towards his own lines, with the Boers in hot pursuit, firing as they rode. A bullet went through Richardson's Stetson hat and two ripped into his tunic.

Just when it looked like he might make it, Sergeant Richardson's horse came up against a three-strand wire fence. Although the two top strands were broken, the bottom one remained intact. It was less than a metre above the ground, but the foam-covered, exhausted horse refused to leap over the single strand.

Meanwhile, the Boers were getting dangerously close and called out for Richardson to surrender. Then a Boer bullet struck the fatigued horse in the shoulder. The startled beast plunged forward, leaped over the wire, and galloped madly towards the Strathcona's. The heroic steed died an hour later from its wounds and exhaustion.

Several officers witnessed Sergeant Richardson's equally heroic rescue. One of them, British Colonel Julian Byng (later commander of the Canadian Corps at the Battle of Vimy Ridge during World War I and governor general from 1921 to 1926) immediately brought the incident to the attention of the British commander-in-chief, Lord Roberts. For his act of gallantry, Sergeant Richardson received the Victoria Cross—the first ever awarded to a member of a formed Canadian unit.

Lieutenant-Colonel Steele took great care to teach his men how to scout safely, without taking undue risks. He remained a strict disciplinarian, busting incompetent sergeants and blasting careless officers. He banned campfires, saying a cup of tea was not worth death or injury. Under artillery barrages, he was the very model of coolness, retiring behind an anthill to light up his pipe.

Meanwhile, Lieutenant-General Buller's advance continued at such a leisurely pace that he earned another nickname—"Sitting Bull." His Natal Field Force finally linked up with Lord Roberts' column, but not before Roberts had already entered Pretoria, the capital of the Transvaal.

The loss of their capital city made no difference to the agrarian Boers, and the war now entered a guerrilla phase as they harassed the British and colonial troops in quick hit-and-run attacks. As a result, Strathcona's Horse was in constant demand as scouts or guards as the British marched from place to place in their efforts to subdue the Boers.

On July 30, two Boers claimed that a large group of their comrades at a nearby farmhouse wanted to surrender but wanted their countrymen to think they had been captured. Canadians Lieutenant White-Fraser, Sergeant Parker—the former British army captain—and sixteen troopers, along with two native scouts, were sent out bring them in. As the Strathcona's approached the farm, which was flying a white flag, about seventy concealed Boers opened fire.

Lieutenant White-Fraser fell back in good order, but Sergeant Parker, Private Fred Arnold, and the two scouts were well out in front. When the Boers called on them to surrender, Parker shouted "Never!" He and the scouts were shot dead at close range. Arnold was badly wounded, and died in hospital later.

The Boers' treachery incensed Sergeant Parker's comrades, and they vowed to take revenge. Undoubtedly they did, but the details are unrecorded. Rumours circulated that Strathcona's Horse had lynched Boer prisoners. One story states that when a British staff officer tried to intervene, the troopers offered to string him up, too!

Perhaps this is the origin of the British press's name for the regiment—"The Headhunters." The London *Daily Express* reported, "Of all the regiments, British or Colonial, regular or irregular, Strathcona's Horse among the Boers were the most dreaded, and strange to say, the most respected."

In the third week of August, the forces of Lord Roberts and Lieutenant-General Buller moved together in a pincer movement against Boer General Louis Botha's army in the eastern Transvaal. Buller tried to force his way through the Boer lines with a massive artillery bombardment by forty guns. Mickey McCormick, Lieutenant-Colonel Steele's young trumpeter, witnessed the firepower of the guns, which made "it look like the eruption of Mount Vesuvius, as smoke, dirt, rocks and sulphurous gasses shot up from the position." Although the two arms of the pincer closed, the Boers slipped through its claws. As General Botha escaped north, Lord Roberts issued a proclamation annexing the Transvaal as a British possession.

But a hard core of Boers refused to concede defeat and continued to fight. Strathcona's Horse continued north, in pursuit of Botha's Boers.

It was hard, tiring work for both men and horses, with little to eat and drink and not much time to rest. Such was to be the remainder of the campaign. But it was the type of outdoor existence to which both the experienced horsemen of Strathcona's Horse and the Boer units were accustomed in their prewar lives—whether on grassy prairie or open veldt, gentle foothill or rocky kopje. In fact, there was really not much difference in the way the men who now fought as enemies lived in peacetime.

At the beginning of September, the British advance halted against an entrenched Boer line in a valley that blocked the road to Lydenburg. Over the next couple of days, Strathcona's Horse guarded first one flank and then the other, as Lieutenant-General Buller tried to outflank the Boers. The Strathcona's also placed guards on a high ridge overlooking the Crocodile Valley, through which the British had to pass, until someone ordered them back.

Lieutenant-Colonel Steele became concerned about this lapse in security and sent out a scouting party under Lieutenant John Leckie to ensure that the Boers had not occupied these heights. Once on the ridge, Leckie sent Sergeant Archibald Logan and four men further ahead to occupy a forward post. As they took up their positions, more than a hundred Boers sprang from nearby hiding places and attacked the small patrol. They wounded one man and quickly surrounded the other four, who opened fire in response to the Boers' calls for surrender.

Unfortunately, Lieutenant Leckie and the rest of his men came under attack at the same time and could not help Sergeant Logan and his scouting party. The surrounded Strathcona's took whatever limited cover they could find behind some boulders and resolved to fight it out with the Boers, who were less than a hundred metres away. The Boer leader again called for surrender, but was answered by rifle and revolver fire from the Canadians.

When Lieutenant-Colonel Steele became aware of the situation on the ridge, he sent a detachment of soldiers to the rescue. Sergeant John Brothers (who had made the fortune in the Klondike) and another man were ordered to scout towards Sergeant Logan's position. But the rescuers quickly became involved with the enemy as the fighting intensified. It continued throughout the next day until some British soldiers managed to threaten the Boers' flanks, forcing them to withdraw that evening.

No one survived to tell the story of what happened to the isolated soldiers. The details of their fate were surmised from the positions in which their bodies were found and from the testimony of Boer witnesses. Sergeant Logan and his Strathcona's had held the enemy at bay for several hours until, wounded, bleeding, and out of ammunition, they were finally killed by the Boers.

The next day, the infantry found the dead troopers close together, their bodies riddled by bullets, some with their rifles still at the shoulder. Seventeen dead Boers lay scattered on the ground around them, silent testimony to the Strathcona's Horse regimental motto: Perseverance. The bodies of Sergeant Brothers and his companion were also found. They had put up a valiant fight, killing six Boers with their revolvers before being killed themselves.

The total casualties in Strathcona's Horse were six killed and three wounded; the worst day for the unit. All might have been avoided if the guards had been left on the ridge as good military tactics dictated.

In October the Natal Field Force was broken up and Lieutenant-General Buller left for England. He bade farewell to the unit by telling it, "I have never served with a nobler, braver or more serviceable body of men. It shall be my privilege when I meet my friend, Lord Strathcona, to tell him what a magnificent body of men bear his name."

In the third week of October, Strathcona's Horse was eighty kilometres west of Johannesburg on remounts, moving to assist in the relief of a British brigade besieged at Frederikstad. As the relief column arrived, the blockaded British counter-attacked the now under-strength Boers, supported by a heavy artillery bombardment. The Boers broke and fled across an open field, where many were killed.

After the battle, trumpeter Mickey McCormick walked among the Boer dead that littered the field, when he noticed "a boy younger than himself, a fine looking boy, perhaps not over thirteen years old. His wide open blue eyes looking at the sun." Through an open shirt, "a swarm of flies covered his bloody intestines oozing out of a hole in his navel."

Tears welled up in trumpeter McCormick's eyes as he stood by the boy, brushing the flies away, happy that he "carried no rifle and had no part in the battle. A few metres away, lay another dead Boer, his Mauser rifle beside him [and] his left arm stretched towards the boy." McCormick was convinced the boy was the man's son. The memory of the tragedy of that small scene that had played out on the battlefield stayed with McCormick for the rest of his life.

What followed was the most frustrating and exhausting experience for Strathcona's Horse in South Africa: early reveille, few rations, weary horses, wet days, cold nights, and constant sniper attacks as they tried to run down a band of Boers. In the end, the unit's superhuman efforts were unsuccessful: a major disappointment.

Strathcona's Horse returned to Canada via England. Aboard the ship a British artilleryman, who had served in the same column as the Canadian horsemen, was asked his opinion of the regiment. "Well," he replied, "we could always sleep with our boots off when they were doing the scouting."

As the ship chugged northwards, Queen Victoria died on January 22, 1901, bringing an era to an end.

Chapter 6
Leliefontein

On a sunny day in July 1900, a troop of twenty tired troopers of the Royal Canadian Dragoons rested in an outpost on a small, steep-sided hill, known in South Africa as a kopje. Tall brown grass stretched across the landscape in all directions, rippled by a gentle breeze. Only an occasional thicket of stunted trees interrupted the featureless landscape.

Nearby, a herd of springbok were grazing. The springbok, a small red antelope, is a highly strung, swift, and graceful creature. When startled, a herd might bound off in nine- to twelve-metre leaps and can easily outrun horses. Hunters claim that when a springbok hears a rifle shot it can leap fast enough to avoid the bullet.

While most of the troopers dozed in the warmth of the midday sun, one man—a keen-eyed sentry—remained alert.

Crouched behind a rock, he was watching the herd, which had stopped grazing and appeared increasingly nervous. The sentry signalled his lieutenant to join him.

"Those deer," he whispered, "something's bothering them, sir. The grass seems to be moving, but it's not the wind."

The officer looked through his binoculars. "Boers!" he exclaimed softly. "The grass is alive with them!" He quietly ordered his men to stand to.

Soon, twenty rifles pointed silently towards the moving grass less than a hundred metres away. Suddenly, fifty Boers leapt to their feet with a shout and charged the hill. The Dragoons opened up simultaneously with rapid fire.

"Troop Front!" Troopers of the Royal Canadian Dragoons train at Winnipeg before their departure for South Africa, 1900.

In seconds most of the Boers lay dead on the ground. Only a few escaped. If it hadn't been for the little springboks' warning, the Canadians would have been wiped out.

After the British occupied the capital of the Transvaal at Pretoria, the Boers adopted guerrilla tactics—making quick raids, damaging communications, hitting supply lines, looting provisions, attacking small detachments, and always slipping away before becoming decisively engaged.

When the weather turned colder—especially at night— the Canadians' light khaki drill uniforms were switched for serge tunics and cord breeches. Clear, bright, sunlight days, frequently accompanied by frost, were common, not unlike perfect fall days in Canada. But fierce thunderstorms could blow up out of nowhere, soaking the horsemen in minutes.

Firewood was difficult to obtain on the high, treeless plains. When some was found, the men carried it in little bundles behind their saddles for the night's fires. But rain often put out the fires that the men brewed their tea over and huddled beside to warm their chilled bones. In any case, the rocky ground held the cold water in large pools, sometimes rendering sleep impossible. Biting wintry winds were a daily occurrence.

Southeast of Pretoria, a detachment of troopers from the Royal Canadian Dragoons under Lieutenants Harold Borden and John Burch rode to the rescue of some Royal Irish Fusiliers under attack by the Boers. The Canadians dismounted, crawled forward, and jumped up to counter-attack the enemy. As they did so, Boer sharpshooters killed the two officers and wounded two men, one so badly that he was blinded. Then the Boers fled. Lieutenants Borden and Burch were the RCD's first fatalities.

Borden was the son of the minister of militia and defence and his death broke his father's spirit. Frederick Borden became convinced that his son's exploits—swimming the Vet River under fire and leading the counter-attack in which he met his death—deserved the Victoria Cross. The denial of even a lesser posthumous award for his son turned Borden's attitudes against the British.

Although a few casualties were caused by Boer action, sickness caused more. On one occasion, Private Ovide Smith of the CMR became ill and reported to the ambulance wagon. The doctor was not around, so the enterprising trooper took matters into his own hands and found a large wicker chest that contained medical supplies.

Printed on a sheet of paper inside the lid was a list of ailments, followed by the diagnosis and a numbered treatment. After reading the sheet, Private Smith concluded he needed a number seven pill. Unfortunately, the number seven bottle was empty, so Smith decided to take a number two and a number five. As Private William Griesbach, later a major-general and senator, noted, "Mathematically he seemed to be dead right, but...we buried him that night."

On one occasion, two RCD troopers foolishly released some captured Boers, along with their rifles and horses, in return for money. When the Boers were later recaptured, they demanded a refund! The two soldiers were sentenced to ten years in prison. In the opinion of their comrades, they got off lightly. Most thought a firing squad would have been more appropriate.

In early July 1900, Field Marshal Lord Roberts ordered the 1st Mounted Infantry Brigade, which included the RCD and CMR, to clear the line of the Delagoa Bay Railroad, running east from Pretoria through Portuguese East Africa to the coast. In mid-July, the Canadian artillery's D Battery of six guns joined the RCD and CMR. The advance began in the third week of July, passing Middelburg, where they encountered light resistance, before moving further east towards Belfast.

In mid-October, newly-promoted Major-General Horace Smith-Dorrien arrived in Belfast to take command, with instructions from Lord Kitchener, who had replaced Lord Roberts as commander-in-chief, to take the battle to the enemy. Smith-Dorrien happily obliged.

In the pre-dawn hours of November 6, Major-General Smith-Dorrien left Belfast and headed south in search of a large group of Boers known as the Carolina commando. He commanded a large force that included the RCD, the CMR, and two 12-pounder guns under Lieutenant Dinky Morrison.

The column, including its wagon train, stretched for ten kilometres across the countryside. Because of sickness, injury, and death—and with no replacement system—the RCD mustered only ninety-five troopers. The CMR was down to sixty.

In contrast to recent cold, wet weather, the sun broke out of an early morning fog and made for a pleasant day. As Boers began to appear, the leading soldiers of the advance guard were able to force them off a series of successive ridges, assisted by Lieutenant Morrison's guns. It was a slow process, and the Boers had time to establish a strong position along a rocky ridge from Witkloof to Leliefontein, overlooking the Komati River.

When the column approached this position, a short engagement followed in which the Canadian gunners supported the British infantry. Major-General Smith-Dorrien ordered Lieutenant-Colonel François Lessard to take the RCD, Morrison's guns, and a detachment of infantry on a wide movement towards Leliefontein to outflank the Boers. When the Boers realized what was happening, they quickly fled south towards Carolina.

That night, Major-General Smith-Dorrien decided to return to Belfast in the morning, using the RCD and the Canadian guns to bring up the tail of the column as the rearguard. In the rearguard, Lieutenant-Colonel Lessard placed his three mounted troops, two 12-pounder artillery guns, and one Colt machine gun in an arc about twenty-five hundred metres wide across the rear of the column.

Lieutenants Hampden Cockburn, Dick Turner, and Francis Sutton commanded the three troops, each split into two twelve- to fifteen-man groups about 460 metres apart. Lieutenant Dinky Morrison's two artillery guns and the Colt machine gun under Sergeant Eddie Holland took up a position in the centre.

The Boers thought the British would advance towards Carolina the next day, and planned to stop them by attacking the column from three sides, preferably during the vulnerable time when the British broke camp. On November 7, the Boers set off early in the morning to carry out their plan.

They soon discovered that Major-General Smith-Dorrien was withdrawing northwards. They would have to improvise. A two-hundred-man Boer force under General Joachim Fourie galloped around to seize a small hill, hoping to cut the line of the British retreat. Lieutenant-Colonel Thomas Evans, now commanding the CMR, got there first with his troopers and held the Boers at bay, assisted by two British guns.

At the same time, a larger Boer force began nipping at the heels of the rearguard, pressing forward in an attempt to find an opening or a weak spot in Lieutenant-Colonel Lessard's group. Once the British main body passed the hill held by the CMR, Lieutenant-Colonel Evans abandoned that position and moved northwards. This freed up a number of

Boers, who joined their comrades harassing the rearguard.

Lessard's movements were tied to the slow pace of the baggage wagons, about five kilometres an hour. In an action repeated many times, one of Lieutenant Morrison's artillery guns would be hooked up to its horse team and race back to the next position. Once it came into action, the second gun galloped back to join it. When both 12-pounders were firing over the RCD troopers' heads, they would mount up and ride to the guns' position.

Suddenly, mounted Boers swooped down on Lieutenant Cockburn's men on the left flank. Lieutenant-Colonel Lessard ordered Morrison with No. 5 gun to his aid. By the time Morrison and the gunners galloped across the 2,500 metres to Lieutenant Cockburn's location, "the horses were rather blown for they had worked hard the previous day."

Lieutenant Morrison described the harrowing scene:

> *Things were certainly hot over there when*
> *we arrived. The Boers were swarming up*
> *from the southwest and coming on with*
> *determination. As we unlimbered and went*
> *into action the Mausers began to incise the*
> *air around us. As our shells began to drift*
> *into the Boers they dismounted and took*
> *cover, but still coming on—rushing from*

cover to cover and firing. I asked Lieut.
Cockburn to extend some more men further
to the front to keep them off the guns until
we put the fear of the Lord into them.

After less than a dozen rounds had been fired, Lieutenant-Colonel Lessard rode over from the other flank. "For God's sake, Morrison," he yelled, "Save your guns!" Pointing to the rear, he shouted again, "Limber up! They're coming down on our flank to cut us off!" As Lessard rode back to the right flank, Lieutenant Cockburn deployed his remaining men to buy time for the artillery guns.

No. 6 gun had already begun to withdraw to the next position when No. 5 limbered up and galloped off. As it did, heavy Mauser fire immediately came from off to the east. Lieutenant Morrison turned to look and "saw a sight the like of which had not been seen before in this war. Square across our rear a line of Boers a mile long was coming on at a gallop over the plain, firing from their horses. It looked like the spectacular finale in a wild west show."

About fifteen hundred mounted Boers hurtled towards him, "coming on rapidly and shooting at our gun, most of them, to try and stop it. I looked up the plain to the ridge we had to reach and I thought indeed we saw our finish."

Lieutenant Cockburn's men were overrun and surrendered, but bought enough time for the artillery gun to get away.

Now only Sergeant Holland's Colt machine gun remained in action. On the right flank, the Dragoons slowly pulled back under heavy fire from the Boers, who now seemed to be pouring in from all directions. Riderless horses stampeded and ran off, adding to the general confusion. Men who had lost their mounts moved back on foot as best they could.

As No. 5 gun made it to the base of a ridge, the exhausted horses slowed to a walk pulling the artillery gun uphill. The Boers were still racing towards it, but Lieutenant Morrison was determined not to lose his gun. He ordered his men into action. A round of shrapnel blew a gap in the Boer line, but did not deter them as they rapidly closed the distance.

In the centre, a few dismounted men under Lieutenant Turner tried to hold off the Boers. As Turner, bleeding from the neck and with a broken arm, posted a few men around Sergeant Holland's Colt machine gun in a shallow depression, he was wounded again and began bleeding profusely.

By now, Major-General Smith-Dorrien had witnessed the desperate fight in which the Dragoons were involved and sent Lieutenant-Colonel Evans and his CMR back to assist. As the reinforcements arrived at the ridge, the Boers commenced their final attempt to capture the artillery guns. General Fourie gathered about a hundred of his Boers and charged the Canadian artillery.

The Boers failed to notice dismounted Dragoons lying in the grass until it was too late. General Fourie was the first to see them. He quickly dismounted and was killed instantly by a bullet through the mouth. Another senior Boer, Commandant Henry Prinsloo, was hit in the head and killed as he tried to warn his men about the dismounted Canadians. The Boers rode through and past the Dragoons, wheeling about to fire from behind.

Sergeant Holland's Colt machine gun jammed with the Boers only a short distance away, close enough to be on him before he would be able to clear it. "I grabbed the gun—which was so hot that it burned my hands—and then I ran for a horse. It was some trouble to get mounted but I managed it and started for the main body...Looking back I saw the Boers take the carriage and turn it towards us. They must have thought they had struck a funny gun."

Most of the Dragoons who had been guarding the machine gun, including Lieutenant Turner, were captured. With the Colt out of action, Lieutenant Morrison realized the Boers would soon be upon his artillery pieces. The gunners dismounted and pulled at the traces to help the spent horses up the ridge.

The Canadians knew if they could only get to the top of the ridge, they would be safe. A large group of British soldiers from the Shropshire Regiment were positioned there to support them. But, to the Canadians' universal horror, they saw the British regulars leaving the battle and disappearing over the ridge instead of providing protective fire. Lieutenant Morrison dashed up and asked their senior officer to help the outnumbered Canadians. Amazingly, he merely replied, "I can't do anything." The British marched away "like automatons," leaving the Canadians to their fate.

The scene was one of utter chaos, as small groups of scattered, outnumbered Canadians desperately fought for their lives. In the confusion, Trooper William Knisley spied his friend Corporal Percy Price, unhorsed, hiding behind a termite mound. Knisley rode across to Price under heavy fire, slung him up behind himself and galloped off, receiving a severe wound in the process.

Just when it seemed all would be lost, Lieutenant-Colonel Evans and the CMR arrived and charged into the advancing Boers. Meanwhile, mounted and dismounted Dragoons made the top of the ridge and spread out to pour fire down at the Boers. By now, the enemy onslaught had begun to slacken. Their two leaders were dead, they had several prisoners to look after, and they had wasted valuable time trying to figure out how to fire the empty Colt machine-gun carriage.

As quickly as they had arrived, the enemy disappeared from the battlefield, leaving three dead and eleven wounded Dragoons. The Canadians in the rearguard moved off and returned to Belfast behind the British column without further incident. The Boers treated their sixteen RCD prisoners well and later released them unharmed.

Leliefontein

On Major-General Smith-Dorrien's recommendation, Lieutenant Dick Turner, Lieutenant Hampden Cockburn, and Sergeant Eddie Holland received the prestigious Victoria Cross, while Lieutenant "Dinky" Morrison (who wrote a book about his experiences entitled *With the Guns in South Africa*) was awarded the Distinguished Service Order, generally regarded as second only to the Victoria Cross when awarded to a junior officer for gallantry. Trooper Bill Knisley was recommended for the Victoria Cross, but received the Distinguished Conduct Medal instead. The award of three Victoria Crosses for the same battle in such a short space of time established a record for gallantry in the annals of Canadian military history that remains unbroken.

Chapter 7
First in the Field

Cecily Jane Georgina Fane Pope was a remarkable woman. Georgina, as she was popularly known, was born in 1862 into a prominent Prince Edward Island family that included a provincial premier and a federal cabinet minister. She studied nursing at New York City's Bellevue Hospital Training School and worked in various American hospitals after graduation.

Within a week of the decision of the Liberal government of Prime Minister Sir Wilfrid Laurier to send a contingent of soldiers to South Africa, many female nurses volunteered their services as auxiliaries in Britain's Royal Army Medical Corps. The Canadian government was prepared to provide them with free passage to South Africa with the Canadian contingent.

The British willingly accepted this offer, while noting—somewhat stuffily—that their own troops could legally be attended only by nurses who belonged to the British Army Reserve, and therefore the numbers of nurses sent to South Africa should not be more than were needed by the colonial contingents. While such an officious rule may have made sense to the bureaucrats who devised it, it would soon be ignored in South Africa.

At the time, the idea of female military nurses was still relatively new. British civilian nurse Florence Nightingale had made history forty-five years earlier, when she led a small party of nurses to Turkey during the Crimean War. Her example paved the road for nursing to be seen as a suitable occupation for young ladies not only in the field, but at home as well.

Canada had used nurses in military operations during the Northwest Rebellion of 1885 and with the Klondike Field Force during the Gold Rush of 1898, but in both cases they were civilians. During the Spanish-American War of 1898, the Americans had also used nursing sisters, and their example was an inspiration to many young women.

The Boer War marked the first time Canada sent uniformed women to war as nurses. Four nurses were chosen from 190 qualified applicants from across Canada and the United States to accompany the Canadian troops. When 2 RCR sailed on the *Sardinian* from Quebec City on October 30, 1899, four nurses were aboard.

Georgina Pope was in charge of this pioneering group of nursing sisters. The other three were Sarah Forbes of Nova

Scotia, and two Ontarians, Minnie Affleck and Elizabeth Russell. Russell had already experienced the rigours of wartime nursing when she served in a hospital ship during the Spanish-American War.

Their khaki nurse's uniform consisted of a bicycle skirt (with a hemline shorter than was fashionable at the time) and a long-sleeved, high-collared Russian-peasant-type blouse with shoulder straps and military buttons, worn with a belt and boots, both of brown leather. Their headdress was a khaki sailor hat with a red brush cockade, or a standard white nursing veil. A white collar, cuffs, and bib apron completed the ensemble.

In South Africa, when 2 RCR was dispatched upcountry, the disappointed sisters were not allowed to accompany them, as nurses could not be accommodated in field hospitals. They were attached instead to the British army's No. 1 General Hospital, a hutted establishment for officers a few kilometres outside of Cape Town at Wynberg. There, the restriction on colonial nurses attending British soldiers was quickly forgotten. A British army doctor noted they were met "with a wildly enthusiastic reception" by the troops.

The Canadian nurses arrived just before the British army's disastrous Black Week of December 1899, and casualties soon came streaming in. Georgina Pope and her three companions worked long hours on crowded wards and were often not able to eat their supper before ten o'clock at night.

94

Although the nurses were inside buildings, working conditions were less than desirable. Bugs infested many of the huts at the Wynberg Hospital. To keep them away from the patients, medical staff placed the legs of the hospital beds in jam tins containing a liquid insecticide.

While female nurses may have been accepted, a Victorian sense of propriety still dictated certain routines. Female nurses were not allowed to remain on the wards for an entire night shift, and could enter only if summoned by a male orderly to see to a patient.

Violating this practice had earned Nightingale the title of "The Lady with the Lamp" in the Crimea, from her habit of checking the hospital wards at night. She was the only woman who was allowed to do this—probably because no man dared to stand up to her once she had made up her mind to do it.

For the Canadian sisters at Wynberg, this restriction meant spending the night in an adjacent shed, appropriately named "The Bunk." When requested by an orderly, a nurse would have to make her way to the appropriate hut—in ankle-deep mud in wet weather.

On Christmas Day, the four Canadian nurses were transferred to a new, tented, 600-bed facility at nearby Rondebosch. No. 3 General Hospital had been hastily erected for other ranks, rather than officers, to assist in looking after the unexpectedly large numbers of casualties from the so-called Black Week.

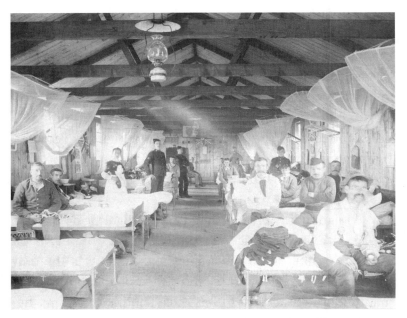

A nursing sister and orderlies supervise a ward at a military hospital in South Africa, 1900. Note the mosquito nets.

The nurses remained there under canvas for over five months, with Sister Pope in charge of a ward for enteric fever victims. According to her, the sisters were "sometimes covered with sand during a 'Cape south-easter,' at others deluged with a forerunner of the coming rainy season, and at all times in terror of scorpions and snakes as bedfellows."

Wounded Canadians soon arrived at Rondebosch, some of the more than 130 RCR casualties from the Battle of Paardeberg. The Canadian nurses greeted them warmly, and considered it a great privilege to look after their injured countrymen.

Meanwhile, Canadian authorities were preparing a second contingent for duty in South Africa. Like the first contingent, this one also consisted of four nursing sisters, selected from the original applicants. Deborah Hurcomb and Margaret Horne were from Montreal, Margaret Macdonald from Nova Scotia, and Marcella Richardson from Regina. Hurcomb was in charge of the group.

The nurses arrived at the end of February 1900, on the same ship as two-thirds of the artillery unit. Sister Macdonald had already worked in a military hospital and on a hospital ship, tending soldiers wounded in Cuba during the Spanish-American War.

During the voyage, the government announced that all nursing sisters would be given the rank of lieutenant, along with the pay and privileges of that grade. Surgeon Lieutenant-Colonel G. Sterling Ryerson, the Canadian commissioner of the Red Cross Society, also had free passage aboard the ship.

The recent arrivals joined the other four nurses at Rondebosch. All shared in the disappointment of not accompanying the newly-arrived Canadian units upcountry. Much of the nurses' work consisted of looking after sick, rather than wounded, soldiers.

Far more soldiers died of disease during the Boer War than from any other cause; only six thousand of the twenty thousand deaths during the conflict were battle casualties. Heat, dust, and flies contributed to much of the illness, but drinking water from polluted sources, leading to dysentery and the ubiquitous enteric fever, caused far more.

Twenty times more soldiers were admitted to hospital for illness than for injuries caused by enemy action or accidents. Enteric fever and dysentery hit 74,000 soldiers, with 8,000 dying of enteric alone. Among the 217 fatal Canadian casualties, over half—some 127—died from various illnesses. In the RCR alone, 350 soldiers eventually caught enteric.

Although the majority of casualties in South Africa were due to illness, thousands of men were injured by enemy fire. When doctors did look after wounded soldiers, they found the wounds were usually "remarkably benign," the result of the high-velocity, small-calibre bullets fired by the Boers' Mauser rifles.

Soldiers described Mauser wounds as being painless at first, feeling like "being pushed, or tapped with a hammer." One war correspondent even noted, "Death from a Mauser bullet is less painful than the drawing of a tooth. Such at least appears to be the case, speaking generally from apparent evidence, without having the opportunity of collecting the opinions of those who have actually died."

In mid-March 1900, Deborah Hurcomb and her group were sent to Kimberley. There, they worked in a temporary 100-bed hospital in a Masonic Temple. Assisted by British orderlies, they looked after patients who were mostly suffering from dysentery and enteric. Towards the end of April, the sisters were sent from Kimberley to Bloemfontein, where they were attached to No. 10 General Hospital.

It was in Bloemfontein that the nurses began what Sister Hurcomb described as "our hardest work in the country." They had arrived during an epidemic of dysentery and enteric, which afflicted over four thousand soldiers there, including several from the RCR. Many of the medical staff became ill themselves. A shortage of food, water, and medical supplies only made matters worse. All but Sister Margaret Macdonald became sick, Sister Margaret Horne so severely that she had to be invalided home.

In May, No. 3 General Hospital was split in two and moved forward. After six months at Rondebosch, nurses Minnie Affleck and Elizabeth Russell moved to Springfontein in the southern part of the Orange Free State, while nurses Georgina Pope and Sarah Forbes were transferred to Kroonstad. The two nursing sisters at Springfontein found life under canvas much colder than at Rondebosch. On night duty, Sister Affleck noted that the medicine often froze in the glasses as she delivered it to her patients.

At Kroonstad, British troops had recently passed through the town, leaving hundreds of sick and wounded behind. To cope with the large numbers, the British established hospitals in several hotels and churches. Sister Pope was put in charge of a nursing staff consisting of Sister Sarah Forbes and five British nurses at the large Kroonstad Hotel.

Soon 230 patients filled the hospital's beds, almost all stricken with typhoid. As frequently happened, the nurses' arrival had preceded necessary medical supplies and hospital stores. In the interim before they arrived, Sister Pope's friend, Red Cross Commissioner G. Sterling Ryerson was able to provide her with such badly needed items as pyjamas, condensed milk, beef essence, whiskey, and many other medical comforts.

A month later, No. 3 General Hospital's equipment arrived and was set up under canvas near the town. It was June, the beginning of winter in the southern hemisphere, and the nurses suffered from the cold, awakening each morning to find frost lining the insides of their bell tents. Sisters Minnie Affleck and Elizabeth Russell joined sisters Georgina Pope and Sarah Forbes at Kroonstad in early July. Then they all moved again, this time to Pretoria.

In mid-July, Sister Deborah Hurcomb and her two remaining nurses were also sent to Pretoria. All seven Canadian nurses worked in the Irish Hospital, where their patients included a number of their countrymen. Field

Marshal Lord Roberts had personally—and considerately—arranged the transfer to allow the nurses to see the Transvaal capital before their tour of duty ended.

In November, the nurses were given a short period of leave before travelling by train to Cape Town. Due to a cut in the rail line they missed the boat carrying the RCR, which they were supposed to accompany. Consequently, they had to wait another month until mid-December, when they embarked on the *Roslyn Castle* with the homeward-bound second contingent.

Their nursing service continued aboard when several soldiers developed enteric fever, two of them fatally. The ship arrived in Halifax in early January 1901.

In her report to the director general of medical services, Sister Pope noted of the patients, "If we have lessened their suffering as we endeavoured to do, we are amply repaid for the hardships which are necessarily encountered in such a campaign."

In 1902, in addition to a new 2 CMR, Canada sent medical resources in the third contingent. Sister Georgina Pope, seven other nursing sisters, and No. 10 Field Hospital Company were dispatched. The nursing group was made up of four who had served there previously and four new ones. Sisters Eleanor Fortescue, Florence Cameron, Margaret Smith, and Amy Scott joined sisters Pope, Forbes, Hurcomb, and Macdonald.

Although it was intended that the nurses would accompany 2 CMR in the third contingent, the commanding officer insisted there was "absolutely no room" on the ship for nurses. Consequently, they had to sail to England separately before continuing their journey on a British vessel. The nurses arrived in Cape Town in early March 1902.

They took the hospital ship *Orcano* to Durban, and then travelled inland by hospital train to Harrismith. Sister Pope described it as "a very pretty little town, about six thousand feet above sea level, lying between the beautiful blue Drakensberg hills and a fine kopje [small, steep-sided hill] called the Platberg." Although they had hoped to work with the Canadian field hospital, it had been sent to Newcastle. Instead, the sisters formed the nursing staff for No. 18 Stationary Hospital, a 600-bed facility.

The nurses worked there for another twelve weeks, mostly among soldiers with mild cases of enteric. Unfortunately, Sister Hurcomb, who had headed the second group of nurses, was invalided home, the result of enteric caught during her earlier tour in the country. About the same time, Sister Cameron suffered a severe attack of jaundice and was sent to recover in Johannesburg.

At the end of May 1902, the welcome news arrived of the signing of a peace treaty and the end of the conflict. The remaining nurses returned to Cape Town and sailed for Canada. They accompanied 2 CMR and 10th Field Hospital aboard the *Winifredian*, arriving in Halifax on July 22.

Chapter 8
A Desperate Last Battle

In South Africa, the British established the first concentration camps in history, to house Boer families that they had cleared from the countryside. It was an attempt to deny supplies for the enemy, as well as to eliminate a source of their intelligence.

Once families were taken from their farms, the British burned their houses, outbuildings, and crops in a ruthless scorched-earth policy. Livestock were shot or herded away. Conditions in the camps were appalling—twenty-seven thousand Boer women and children perished in them.

By August 1900, Boer resistance had been ground down to about twenty-five thousand so-called "bitter enders"—stubborn farmers who were prepared to fight on. They were without artillery and lacked much of the material support that the early Boer units possessed. The British had imprisoned about thirty thousand of their comrades, and most of their families languished in the concentration camps.

To limit the Boers' mobility, the British erected a small fort or blockhouse about every twenty-five hundred metres along rail lines and across the countryside. They strung barbed-wire fences between the blockhouses; a sergeant and a few men manned each one.

By the end of the war, fifty thousand soldiers occupied eight thousand such posts, with another twenty thousand garrisoning several towns. These moves freed up the mounted infantry—nearly eighty thousand men—to chase the Boers instead of patrolling the rail lines.

Once the second contingent (consisting of the RCD, CMR, and artillery) and Strathcona's Horse returned home in late 1900, there were no formed Canadian units left in South Africa. But by November, with the guerrilla phase of the war still dragging on, the British authorities had a request. This time they wanted a large mounted infantry unit, consisting of six hundred men divided into four squadrons. The British were so anxious to have such a unit that they even offered to pay all the costs of raising it.

The response in Canada was so overwhelming that two more squadrons were raised, resulting in a 901-man regiment of six squadrons. A captain commanded each squadron of four thirty-two-man troops, with each troop led by a lieutenant. The name chosen for the new unit was the 2nd Regiment, Canadian Mounted Rifles, or 2 CMR.

Command of the unit fell upon Lieutenant-Colonel Thomas Evans, who had done a fine job in charge of the original CMR in the second contingent. Evans was considered to be Canada's best mounted officer. Many of the officers and a quarter of the men he selected for 2 CMR had previous service in South Africa, such as Mickey McCormick, Lieutenant-Colonel Steele's trumpeter in Strathcona's Horse.

All sorts of men joined the unit, some of them unsavoury characters. Undoubtedly the worst was Walter Gordon, whose real name was John Gray. Gordon was a wanted man. He had killed two men in Assiniboine, stolen their money—plus a team of horses and a wagon—and crossed into the United States.

There, Gordon joined the army, fought in the Spanish-American War, and returned to western Canada. Unfortunately for Gordon, one of his fellow troopers in 2 CMR was a NWMP constable who remembered his face from a wanted poster. Gordon was arrested, tried, found guilty, and hanged for the murders.

The unit used standard British army equipment, although the distinctive Stetson that the other Canadian mounted infantry wore was retained. While privates in the first contingent received a meagre 50¢ a day, those in 2 CMR received $1.24. The period of enlistment this time was for twelve months.

On arrival in South Africa, the unit immediately undertook a two-day train journey to Klerksdorp, southwest of Johannesburg. Travelling in open boxcars under the intense African summer sun was hard on man and beast. The slippery iron floors caused several horses to fall, injuring many and killing quite a few.

While lines of blockhouses and wire stretched across much of the countryside, some areas did not have any. The western Transvaal, a sparsely settled, desert-like region, was one of them. In its vast openness, Boer General Koos de la Rey and three thousand men were still at large. Early in the year, de la Rey had beaten two British columns and captured their commander, Lord Methuen. The new British commander-in-chief, Lord Kitchener, was determined to run de la Rey into the ground.

Lord Kitchener sent thirteen columns totalling sixteen thousand men after the Boers. The Canadians joined Lieutenant-Colonel George Cookson's column, part of a force commanded by Brigadier-General Walter Kitchener (Lord Kitchener's brother) at Klerksdorp.

On an early evening in March, Cookson and his men set off. The column was one of four ordered to make a sixty-five-kilometre night march northwards, turn east, and try to trap the Boers against the Schoon Spruit blockhouse line.

The column travelled light, without wagons or ambulances. Each man carried a half ration consisting of hardtack and canned meat, as well as nearly three kilograms of oats for his horse and 180 rounds of ammunition. Greatcoats and blankets were left behind.

The moon provided enough light for the horses to travel at a fast trot, occasionally breaking into a gallop. A few stumbled in animal burrows and went down, unable to continue, while others could not maintain the pace. Stragglers were left behind.

By three o'clock, the column reached the Witpoort Ridge and Lieutenant-Colonel Cookson deployed his units into formation. Lieutenant-Colonel Evans and half of 2 CMR were spread out along the southern part of the ridge for four kilometres, while his deputy commanded the other half as part of the reserve.

Just as dawn was beginning to break, Mickey McCormick, now seventeen and a bugler, pointed out to Lieutenant-Colonel Evans some wagons in a clearing about fifteen hundred metres behind the British line. The commanding officer dispatched some scouts, who discovered a Boer advance party. A short firefight resulted in three enemy casualties—two dead and one wounded. Leaving half his force to deal with the Boers, Evans moved on with the other half.

About seven o'clock, after several hours of riding into the rising sun, the scouts came across a guarded wagon train. When the firing died down the Canadians had captured three Boers, nine wagons and carts, and a hundred head of cattle. But the rest of the day did little to improve the morning's score.

The advance halted at five-thirty that afternoon. The CMR had one slightly wounded and twenty-two missing—most of them because they had been unhorsed during the night. The majority of the latter found their way to the camp or were found by the troops, "sitting disconsolately on ant heaps or in the shelter of low bushes, stripped of uniforms and equipment and some quite naked."

Soldiers of the 2nd Canadian Mounted Rifles ride across the Trasvaal plains in February and March 1902, searching for the last of the Boers—the so-called "bitter-enders".

The Boers had captured them and, desperately in need of their clothing and equipment, had taken everything, although they were unable to look after them as prisoners. A CMR sergeant-major later captured one of these Boers, a suspicious-looking individual dressed in a Canadian uniform, who was trying to get back to his own lines by pretending to be Canadian. Within two days all of the missing Canadians made it back to their camp.

During the night, several Boers slipped through gaps in the line of horsemen and headed west, where, along the Great Harts River, about twenty-five hundred Boers formed defensive encampments.

By the time the exhausted mounted troops returned to their camp, they had ridden an amazing 140 kilometres and been in the saddle for twenty-three hours. In all-too-typical South African fashion, a thunderstorm had broken out, drenching the troops for the last two hours.

After three days of rest and replenishment, they hit the saddle again. Acting on the barest and often conflicting intelligence, Brigadier-General Kitchener now dispatched his columns westwards. Lieutenant-Colonel Cookson's eighteen-hundred-man force was to follow the course of a streambed, known as Brak Spruit, from its source to its junction with the Great Harts River, a distance of about sixty-five kilometres.

In two days, the British force was at Driekuil, eighty kilometres west of Klerksdorp, where Brak Spruit began. At one in the morning on the last day of March, Lieutenant-Colonel Cookson's men scrambled out of their bedrolls, wolfed down a hasty breakfast, saddled their horses, and rode westwards in the moonlight. The CMR scouts under Lieutenant Casey Callaghan formed part of the advance guard, while half the unit escorted the supply wagons and the remainder was in the main body with their commanding officer, Lieutenant-Colonel Evans.

Around ten o'clock, two of Lieutenant Callaghan's scouts found a fresh trail made by about five hundred men and two guns, heading generally northeast towards the junction of the Little Harts and Great Harts rivers. A dust cloud low in the sky indicated the Boer column was only a few kilometres away.

Lieutenant-Colonel Cookson ordered Lieutenant-Colonel Evans to stay behind and wait for the wagons to catch up, while he led the rest of the column—perhaps fifteen hundred men—in pursuit of the fleeing Boers. The sixty-man advance guard, made up of Damant's Horse (an irregular unit) and the CMR scouts, galloped at full speed along a trail beside Brak Spruit. Five kilometres down the trail, they ran into a Boer ambush.

The Boers had posted a strong rearguard in the bushes on either side of the trail, near a farmhouse. Within minutes, the enemy killed two of Lieutenant Callaghan's scouts and wounded nine others, and also killed fifteen horses. In their eagerness to catch the Boers, the Canadians had been careless and paid for it dearly. Fortunately, the main body appeared and the Boers beat a hasty retreat to rising ground on both sides of the streambed near two farms, one of which was called Boschbult.

By now, Lieutenant-Colonel Cookson had advanced thirty kilometres from Driekuil and the number of Boers he was pursuing had grown to about twenty-five hundred men—larger than his eighteen-hundred-man force—led by some of the Boers' best leaders. The enemy also held the high ground and had good cover. Cookson had no choice but to hold his position around the farms, stretching down to the streambed. He was not strong enough to attack, and to go back might have led to a difficult running fight with the larger Boer force.

Lieutenant-Colonel Cookson placed about two hundred men out in front of his position to protect the farm area while the British fed their horses and had lunch. No thought was given to preparing defences or to scouting the surrounding countryside. About noon, Lieutenant-Colonel Evans and 2 CMR rode up with the wagons, an impressively long line of horsemen visible through the dust cloud they stirred up. The Boers held back—watching, counting the British and Canadians—and waiting until the time was right to attack.

It came less than two hours later. By now, the wagons had formed a defensive circle and been wired together, while the horses and mules were tethered in the protection of the streambed at the rear of the position.

As the Canadians started to prepare defences, Lieutenant-Colonel Cookson ordered the two detachments on his left flank closer to his position and sent two hundred British mounted rifles and a pom-pom gun to a farmhouse about 550 metres to the east. The protective element to the north was also reduced by pulling most of its units back to Boschbult.

A detachment under Lieutenant Bruce Carruthers had been the rearguard for the wagon escort. As they approached the British position, Carruthers realized that it might be better to remain where he was, protecting the open flank at the rear. Lieutenant-Colonel Evans concurred. Carruthers kept twenty men with him, and sent Sergeant Hodgins and a smaller party a few hundred metres to his right.

Sometime after one in the afternoon, the Boers began shelling the British with four captured artillery guns and a pom-pom. From positions on the surrounding ridges, their riflemen fired into the British position and at the tethered animals. There had not yet been enough time to dig any trenches, so men and beasts were hit from all sides. The animals and their civilian drivers panicked, causing greater confusion and hindering the digging of trenches.

In a departure from their previous tactics, the Boers made repeated mounted attacks against the camp over the next few hours. Around half past three, Lieutenant-Colonel Cookson ordered the troops protecting the north side back into the camp.

The Boers moved in as soon as they noticed these soldiers—a large number of mounted infantrymen and Lieutenant Carruthers' two mounted detachments—starting to move. Most of the British pulled back in good order, but those on the east broke and fled—a stampede, in Evans's terms.

Lieutenant Carruthers's small command, by now reduced to twenty-one men, was all that blocked the Boers from riding into the position from the rear. The Canadians held their ground, lying in the grass and firing against tremendous odds until their ammunition was exhausted. When the Boers eventually overran the position, seventeen Mounted Rifles had been killed or wounded. The Boers took the survivors about three kilometres away, where they removed their clothing and equipment.

Lieutenant-Colonel Evans's account of the courageous actions of the small party reflects the intensity of the engagement:

> *Sergt. Perry, although badly wounded,*
> *fought until he was killed. Corporal*
> *Wilkinson, shot twice through the arm*
> *and body, continued fighting until he was*
> *shot through the eye. He then threw the*
> *bolt of his rifle into the long grass to render*
> *it useless to the enemy. Private Evans,*
> *although mortally wounded through the*

bowels, exhausted his ammunition, secured another bandolier, used it up, and, as the Boers were making their final rush, he broke his rifle rendering it useless. Private Evans died shortly after being brought into camp. Private Minchin, although wounded in six places, fired his last shot when the Boers were only 25 yards off, and then threw his bolt into the grass.

In summing up the gallant action, Lieutenant-Colonel Evans wrote, "The splendid stand made by Lieut. Carruthers's party without cover of any kind, and against overwhelming odds, was well worthy of the best traditions of Canada and the whole Empire." That it was.

Around five o'clock the Boers suddenly stopped firing. The British and Canadians continued their defensive preparations in anticipation of a night attack, but, for some unknown reason, the Boers did not attack that night. In the morning, a few could be seen on nearby ridges, but they soon disappeared. The column's ordeal was over.

At eleven the next morning, Lieutenant-Colonel Evans conducted a brief burial service for his dead troopers in a downpour. About two hours later, a relief force arrived from Driekuil. Brigadier-General Kitchener had waited until daylight because a few drivers and mounted infantry who had escaped from Boschbult told him that Lieutenant-Colonel Cookson's force was destroyed. An earlier arrival of these reinforcements could have turned the defeat into a victory.

A few days later, the CMR discovered what had happened to six of their missing mates. Corporal Bill Knisley (who had saved a comrade's life at Leliefontein by riding through heavy Boer fire to rescue him) and five privates had been cut off when the Boers overpowered Lieutenant Carruthers and his men. When Knisley realized they would not be able to make it back into the main position, he headed for Klerksdorp.

His small party rode eastwards all night, stopping occasionally to rest their horses. The next day four Boers attacked them, but the Canadians succeeded in getting away after dark.

The next morning, with the Boers still in pursuit, Knisley and his men took refuge on a stony hill, where they built a hasty defensive position of rocks. A group of fifty Boers appeared shortly, following the exhausted troopers' trail. The greatly outnumbered Canadians held the enemy at bay for five hours. Then, with Knisley and a private dead, ammunition short, and the Boers within 180 metres, the four survivors surrendered.

The Boers respectfully joined the Canadians in a burial service for their two dead comrades, then stripped them to their underwear and released them. They also removed the clothing from the bodies of Knisley and the dead trooper, but thoughtfully buried Knisley's Distinguished Conduct Medal and Queen's South Africa Medal ribbon with him. Two days later, the four surviving troopers walked into Klerksdorp, some 110 kilometres from Boschbult—tired, hungry, and with blistered feet.

Total British losses at the Battle of Harts River were 33 killed, 126 wounded, and more than 70 missing. For the Canadians, Harts River was a bloody battle—second only to the first day at Paardeberg in terms of casualties: 11 killed, 43 wounded, and 7 missing, plus 121 horses and 22 mules killed. Coming as late as it did in the war, it gave the British momentary cause for concern but ultimately had no effect on their final victory.

Epilogue
Home at Last

Now, more than a century after the fighting ended, the Boer War is no longer a part of living memory. As one of Britain's many colonial wars, its relatively small encounters were soon overshadowed by the larger, horrendous battles of the First World War, to be followed within a generation by the major campaigns of the Second World War. Yet, at the time, the Boer War was the single most important event for Canadians—both those who supported the war, and those who opposed it.

Today, there are only a few reminders of that far-off war, largely in the form of group and individual war memorials in various cities and towns across the country. Although a few monuments commemorating earlier conflicts—such as the Seven Years' War (1756–63), the War of 1812, the Fenian Raids of the late 1860s, and the Northwest Rebellion of 1885—had been raised earlier, the Boer War inspired the first widespread erection of memorials to the fallen in Canada.

Among the group memorials are those in Halifax (where there are two), Quebec City, Montreal (specifically to Strathcona's Horse), Ottawa, Toronto, Brantford, London, Windsor, and Calgary. A few towns and villages erected statues to individual soldiers, possibly the last time that communities did this. At the time, it was still inexpensive enough to do so, especially with one or two soldiers coming from an area that encompassed several towns and villages. In a population much smaller than today's, many families knew each other and the impact of battlefield deaths inspired fellow citizens to contribute the necessary funds.

One such individual memorial is to Harold Borden in Canning, Nova Scotia. He was the son of the minister of militia and defence and perhaps the country's most famous casualty of the war. In Granby, Quebec, a statue honours William Latimer, the first battlefield death of the Royal Canadian Artillery. Another monument to a single soldier stands in Cayuga, Ontario, in honour of Bill Knisley. Knisley received the Distinguished Conduct Medal for his actions at Leliefontein, but was killed after the Battle of Harts River while trying to escape from the Boers.

On a personal level, my introduction to the Boer War occurred soon after I was commissioned as a lieutenant into the Royal Canadian Dragoons in 1966. That summer, when I joined my unit in Camp Gagetown, New Brunswick, I was quickly indoctrinated into the stories of the Dragoons' deeds in that war, especially their remarkable performance at Leliefontein on the morning of November 7, 1900. In that short, sharp clash, three members of the regiment earned Victoria Crosses in a fiercely-fought rearguard action to protect two attached artillery guns.

When I joined the Dragoons, there were still a few living veterans of the Boer War. Dick Turner, one of the three Victoria Cross recipients, had died only five years earlier, less than a month short of his ninetieth birthday. Amazingly, the last British Empire veteran of the Boer War did not die until 1993. George Frederick Ives had served in the British army, immigrated to Canada after the war, and settled in British Columbia, where he lived until his death at 111 years of age.

The Royal Canadian Dragoons honour the Battle of Leliefontein annually on its November anniversary and I was quickly caught up in the planning and rehearsals for "Leliefontein Weekend"—an extensive programme of events, including a dismounted parade and inspection by the colonel of the regiment, a mounted rollpast in our Centurion tanks, a memorial church service, inter-ranks sports games, and a formal dinner in the officers' mess.

In these various ways the stories of the Dragoons' achievements continue to be told to new soldiers and officers when they join the unit, inculcating in them pride in the heroic deeds of their forebears and contributing to the esprit de corps and the morale of the unit today.

Later, when I was transferred to Lord Strathcona's Horse (Royal Canadians), I learned entirely new stories about the Boer War and the unit that had been formed expressly to fight in that war. Like the Dragoons, the Strathcona's foster a deep pride in the accomplishments of their predecessors on the high South African plains. Tales of Sam Steele's remarkable leadership, "Tappy" Richardson's Victoria Cross, and the unit's reputation as rough-and-ready "Soldiers of the Queen" are told and retold with a mixture of pride and awe.

The Strathcona's ensure that every new soldier and officer who joins the unit is made fully aware of these deeds. In due course, first as a squadron commander, and then a few years later as the Strathcona's commanding officer, it was one of my own major responsibilities to ensure that the traditions and esprit de corps established by the unit in South Africa were remembered and fostered.

On a wider level, the South African or Boer War of 1899–1902 marked the first foreign deployment of Canadian troops, setting a pattern that would be repeated several times during the twentieth century. The war marked a number of other firsts for Canada: the first member of a formed Canadian unit to earn the Victoria Cross, the first deployment of an Army Field Hospital, and the first employment of women in wartime as nurses.

A parade at Ottawa's parliament buildings marks the return of the Royal Canadian Regiment from South Africa, November 3, 1900.

Major-General Smith-Dorrien said of the Royal Canadian Regiment, "There are no finer or more gallant troops in all the world." When the RCR returned home, Canada's first unit to go into battle overseas was disbanded. Although 2 RCR was no more, its permanent force parent perpetuates its record of service. At a cost of 68 dead and 115 wounded, two more battle honours (Paardeberg and South Africa 1899–1900) had been added to the regiment's list. In honour of that first overseas battle, the RCR still celebrates Paardeburg Day annually.

Lieutenant-Colonel William Otter, the RCR commanding officer, was promoted to colonel just before leaving South Africa and was made a Companion of the Bath for his service there. He was later knighted and became only the second full general Canada ever promoted.

When the RCR's medical orderly Dick Thompson was nominated for the Queen's Scarf, he was in England recovering from sunstroke and rheumatism. He eventually received the scarf in July 1900—by registered mail! It was an inexcusable way to present what is perhaps the rarest decoration ever awarded to any Canadian.

He returned to South Africa and served as a lieutenant in the paramilitary South African Constabulary for a year. He died prematurely of acute appendicitis in 1908.

After Thompson's death, the scarf was sent to his brother in Cork, Ireland, where the family proudly displayed it, but somehow it ended up being put into a trunk in an attic in the 1930s, apparently lost to history. Eventually, though, in 1964 some dedicated researchers did locate it and arranged for its return to Canada. It is still there today, on display in the Canadian War Museum in Ottawa.

Bill Hart-McHarg returned to British Columbia, rejoined his militia unit, and rose steadily through the ranks. He wrote about his experiences in *From Quebec to Pretoria with the*

Royal Canadian Regiment, one of the few personal Canadian accounts of the war.

On the outbreak of World War I, he was promoted to lieutenant-colonel and commanded the 7th (British Columbia) Battalion, Canadian Expeditionary Force. On April 24, 1915, he was killed in his unit's first major action of the war at the Second Battle of Ypres, in Belgium. In the 1950s, a mountain peak in the Rockies was named in his honour.

J. Hilliard Rorke returned from South Africa as a corporal, resumed his journalistic career, and retained his militia connections. During World War I, he commanded the 248th Battalion, Canadian Expeditionary Force, one of the battalions that the Grey Regiment raised for the war. The unit never made it into action, but was broken up to provide reinforcements for the Canadian Corps in Europe.

Major-General Smith-Dorrien had witnessed much of the gallant action of the Royal Canadian Dragoons rearguard at Leliefontein personally, describing it as "an event unprecedented in this war." The British general claimed "he would choose no other mounted troops in the world before [the RCD and CMR], if he had his choice."

It was on his recommendation that Lieutenants Dick Turner and Hampden Cockburn, as well as Sergeant Eddie Holland, received the Victoria Cross, and Trooper Bill Knisley received the Distinguished Conduct Medal. The award of three Victoria Crosses for the same battle in such a short space of time established a record of gallantry in the annals of Canadian military history that remains unbroken.

Of the three RCD Victoria Cross recipients, Dick Turner remained in the militia and on the outbreak of World War I was promoted to brigadier-general in command of 3rd Infantry Brigade. He fought at the Second Battle of Ypres, where the Germans used poison gas for the first time, and later commanded 2nd Canadian Division as a major-general. He was knighted, promoted to lieutenant-general, and put in command of all Canadian troops in England.

After the Boer War, Hampden Cockburn became a major in Toronto's Governor General's Bodyguard, a militia cavalry unit. He later moved to Saskatchewan, where he was killed in a riding accident on his ranch in 1913. Eddie Holland was commissioned in his old unit, Ottawa's Princess Louise Dragoon Guards. During World War I, he commanded a Canadian motor machine-gun unit, one of the world's first.

Lieutenant-Colonel François Lessard remained as commanding officer of the Dragoons until 1907, when he was promoted colonel and made the army's adjutant general. Many felt he should have been given command of the 1st Canadian Division on the outbreak of World War I (it was given to a British officer), but Sam Hughes, the controversial and opinionated minister of militia and defence, would not allow a French Canadian or a Roman Catholic in command.

Instead, Lessard was made inspector general for Eastern Canada, with the rank of major-general.

In appreciation of the springboks' saving RCD lives by warning them of the Boers' approach, the Dragoons adopted the graceful little antelope as their official cap and collar badges. Soldiers of the regiment still proudly wear the springbok today.

After the war, Lieutenant "Dinky" Morrison, who commanded the two artillery guns at Leliefontein and received the Distinguished Service Order (generally regarded as second only to the Victoria Cross when awarded to a junior officer for gallantry), returned to his journalistic career and wrote a book based on his experiences entitled *With the Guns in South Africa*. He became editor-in-chief of the *Ottawa Citizen*, while maintaining his militia connections. During World War I, Morrison commanded senior artillery formations in action, became a major-general, and was knighted for his services.

Although Strathcona's Horse was disbanded after the war, the stories of the deeds they accomplished under the most trying of conditions lived on. In honour of their exploits in South Africa, the government re-established Strathcona's Horse as a unit of the permanent force in 1909.

The Strathcona's Horse Victoria Cross recipient, Sergeant Arthur "Tappy" Richardson, returned to the Mounties, was promoted to sergeant-major, married, and had a daughter. His life then commenced a downward spiral; it seemed the fame of his rare award was more than he could handle. He believed that his medal entitled him to a commission, went heavily into debt, and eventually suffered ill health.

In 1907 he resigned from the RCMP and became the town constable for Indian Head, Saskatchewan. But he held that position for only a short time before losing it for financial and health reasons. Apparently, both he and his wife had become addicted to opium, a drug easily obtained at the time. The townspeople supported him for a while, until he returned to his native Liverpool, England, in 1908.

After his wife died, Richardson spent his remaining sixteen years in obscurity, holding a number of labourer's jobs. He did not even make his whereabouts known to his mother and other relatives.

While Richardson preferred anonymity, someone else did not. A namesake in Scotland impersonated him and received the honours due a Victoria Cross recipient on several occasions. That Arthur Richardson even attended a garden party for Victoria Cross holders at Buckingham Palace, hosted by King George V. His fake identity was not discovered until he had been given a military funeral after his death in 1924.

On learning this, the real Arthur Richardson spoke up and exposed the now-dead impostor. He was also reunited with his family. When Richardson died in 1932 at the age of fifty-nine, the Victoria Cross hero was buried with full military honours in Liverpool's St. James' Cemetery.

Home at Last

The commanding officer of Strathcona's Horse, Lieutenant-Colonel Sam Steele, became a senior commander in the South African Constabulary. After five years he returned to Canada, joined the permanent force, and commanded Strathcona's Horse for a second time, from 1910 to 1912. On the outbreak of World War I, he was promoted to major-general and took the 2nd Canadian Division to England. When the division went to France, because of his age Steele was kept in England in an administrative capacity. He was knighted in 1918 and died a year later.

The Canadian nursing sisters had acquired an excellent reputation for fine teamwork during their service in South Africa. Sister Georgina Pope's important role during the war was recognized in 1903, when she received the Royal Red Cross for "conspicuous service in the field," the first Canadian to earn this high honour.

One of Pope's nursing companions, Margaret Macdonald, later became matron-in-chief of the Canadian Nursing Service in 1914 and paid tribute to Pope's role in South Africa:

> *Surely nowhere at the outset could there*
> *have been a nurse better qualified or so*
> *well fitted for the work in hand. Along*
> *with splendid organizing ability and*
> *fine social background, was combined a*
> *charming personality and ready wit that*

*had a good understanding of the good
qualities, as well as the shortcomings, of
[the British soldier]. Generous in all her
dealings, Miss Pope hated wasteful methods
of work; she dignified menial tasks and
made it something one longed to do. She
delighted in the entertainment of all soldier
patients, but could be stern when occasion
demanded.*

In later life, Georgina Pope once remarked, "...the sight of soldiers or sailors marching, a bugle call, the sound of drums or military band has power to stir in me the old enthusiasm and once more I long to minister to such cheery, grateful patients as the Soldiers and Sailors of the King."

After the war, Sister Pope remained as a reserve nurse until 1906, when she was appointed to the Halifax Military Hospital. In 1908, she became the first matron of the Canadian Army Medical Corps, an appointment she held for the next six years.

On Georgina Pope's recommendation, the nurses' khaki uniform was changed to blue, resulting in the nickname "bluebirds," by which Canadian nursing sisters were affectionately known during World War I. When that war broke out, Sister Pope was fifty-two years old. She went overseas and served with Canadian hospitals in England

and France before being invalided home due to illness just as the war ended.

Despite her war disability, Georgina Pope lived in retirement to the age of seventy-six, dying in her Prince Edward Island home in June 1938. After lying in state in Government House, she was buried with full military honours. Seventy military and civilian nurses led her funeral procession, which included many veterans of the Boer War and World War I. In November 2006, she was honoured again, as one of only two women in "The Valiants," fourteen statues of Canadian war heroes in Ottawa's Confederation Square.

When the Boer War started, hardly anyone in Britain expected a handful of mere farmers to defeat the most experienced regular army in the world on several occasions and to hold it off for three years. In the end, it took nearly half a million of the Empire's soldiers to finally subdue perhaps forty thousand Boers in what became history's first modern conflict.

Compared with the British commitment of about 450,000 men, Canada's effort was relatively small. Of the 7,368 Canadians who served in South Africa, 89 were killed in action, 135 died of disease, and 252 were wounded. Canadians—and others—believed that their units sent to South Africa did extremely well there. Largely made up of citizen soldiers, the units discovered that they more than measured up satisfactorily against tough British regulars.

While many Canadians undoubtedly went to South Africa in search of adventure, many instead found a harsh climate, continuous hunger and thirst, assorted diseases, and, for a few, injury or death. But those who survived returned with a distinct pride in being Canadian, and a new sense of confidence in their ability to function effectively as soldiers. Canada's commitment also deepened the rift between English and French Canada, a division that was to have severe consequences when it came to finding enough volunteers to fight in the two world wars that followed.

The RCR was credited with the lion's share of the victory at Paardeberg, while the mounted rifles units were clearly recognized as being among the best on the British side. The experience of fighting together in the war taught the Canadians a number of important lessons that carried over into militia training back in Canada.

During the longer and larger bloodbaths that followed in the twentieth century, Canadian soldiers upheld the first-class reputation that their predecessors so deservedly earned in South Africa during the Boer War—Canada's first overseas conflict.

Bibliography

Barnes, Col. Ian, ed. *Strathcona's Horse: South Africa 1900–1901*. Calgary: Bunker to Bunker, 2000.

Fraser, W. B. *Always a Strathcona*. Calgary: Comprint Publishing, 1976.

Greenhous, Brereton. *Dragoon: The Centennial History of the Royal Canadian Dragoons, 1883–1983*. Ottawa: Guild of the Royal Canadian Dragoons, 1983.

Hart-McHarg, William. *From Quebec to Pretoria with the Royal Canadian Regiment*. Toronto: Briggs, 1902.

Marquis, T. G. *Canada's Sons on Kopje and Veldt*. Toronto: Canada's Sons Publishing, 1900.

Miller, Carman. *Painting the Map Red: Canada and the South African War, 1899–1902*. Montreal: McGill-Queen's University Press, 1993.

Morrison, E. W. B. *With the Guns in South Africa*. Hamilton: Spectator Printing, 1901.

Morton, Desmond. *The Canadian General, Sir William Otter*. Toronto: Hakkert, 1974.

Nicholson, G. W. L. *Canada's Nursing Sisters*. Toronto: Hakkert, 1975.

Reid, Brian A. *Our Little Army in the Field: The Canadians*

in South Africa, 1899–1902. St. Catherine's: Vanwell
  Publishing, 1996.
Stewart, Robert. *Sam Steele, Lion of the Frontier*. Toronto:
  Doubleday, 1979.
Worthington, Larry. *The Spur and the Sprocket*.
  Kitchener: Reeve Press, 1968.

Acknowledgements

Of all the assistance I received in writing this book, no one was more helpful than Joyce Glasner, a former east coast consulting editor for *Amazing Stories*. She is a fellow writer as well, and has a number of *Amazing Stories* to her credit.

A luncheon arranged by a mutual friend resulted in a fortuitous meeting with Audrey Ogilvie. She kindly allowed me to share with a wider audience the letters of J. Hilliard Rorke, her maternal grandfather, who served with the RCR throughout the Boer War. The contents of Hilliard's letters home have never been made public before, and his insights, opinions, and comments provide a fresh—and surprisingly mature—outlook on the ordinary soldiers' experiences.

Few, if any, works of non-fiction are written in isolation. Most of them draw, to one degree or another, on the research and writings of others. This book is certainly no exception, and I am indebted to several authors who have written about the Boer War, especially since the last veterans of that far-off conflict passed away several years ago. I have listed my main sources in the bibliography.

During my research, I made frequent use of the wonderful book collection at Halifax's Cambridge Military Library, and would like to thank librarian Jeanne Howell and custodian

Sergeant Michaela Brister for their outstanding help, as usual. I have used all the books listed in the bibliography for quotes included in this book and would like to formally acknowledge these sources.

Finally, I must thank publisher Jim Lorimer and his team for their efforts in bringing this book to print. This includes the *Amazing Stories* series editor, Nancy Sewell, Formac managing editor Christen Thomas, copy editor Laurie Miller, and the production team of Andrew Herygers and Meredith Bangay.

About the Author

John Boileau served in the Canadian army for thirty-seven years, retiring as a colonel in 1999. During his armoured corps career he served in various command, staff, and training appointments across Canada and abroad. His foreign tours included several postings to Great Britain, with NATO forces in Germany, in the United States, and on United Nations peacekeeping duty in Cyprus. He served as a troop leader and adjutant of the Royal Canadian Dragoons, as well as a squadron commander and commanding officer of Lord Strathcona's Horse (Royal Canadians).

In retirement, John has pursued a lifelong interest in history by writing about it. He has had nearly three hundred historical articles published in numerous Canadian and American magazines and newspapers, and contributes regularly to several publications. He is the author of eight other books: *Fastest in the World: The Saga of Canada's Revolutionary Hydrofoils; Half-Hearted Enemies: Nova Scotia, New England and the War of 1812; Valiant Hearts: Atlantic Canada and the Victoria Cross; Samuel Cunard: Nova Scotia's Master of the North Atlantic; Where the Water Meets the Land: The Story of the Halifax Harbour Waterfront; Historic Eastern Passage; The Peaceful Revolution: 250 Years of Democracy in*

Nova Scotia and *Halifax & The Royal Canadian Navy*. John and his wife, Miriam, live on a small island in St. Margaret's Bay, on Nova Scotia's picturesque South Shore.

Photo Credits

Index

Camp Gagetown, NB,
119
Canadian Army Medical
Corps, 128
Canadian artillery,
54–55, 57–59, 62
Canadian Mounted
Rifles (CMR), 9, 55,
57–60, 62, 82–85, 88,
90, 123
Canadian Nursing
Service, 127
Canning, NS, 118
Cape Colony, 11, 24, 58
Cape Town, 26, 57, 69,
101, 102
Carnarvon, 59
Carnarvon Field Force,
58–59, 62
Carolina, 84, 85
Carolina commando, 83
Carruthers, Lieutenant
Bruce, 112–15
casualties, 46, 49–50,
77, 94–98, 107, 116,
121, 129
C Company, RCR, 15,
17, 30, 44, 46
Cayuga, Ont, 118
Charlottetown, PEI, 15
Clarkson, Corporal
Joseph, 57–58
CMR *see* Canadian
Mounted Rifles
Cockburn, Lieutenant
Hampden, 85–87, 91,
123–24
Colt machine guns, 54,
85, 88
Colt revolvers, 16, 67
commandos, 13
Companion of the Bath,
122
concentration camps,
103–104
Confederation Square,
Ottawa, 129
Cookson, Lieutenant-

Colonel George, 106–
107, 109–12, 115
Cranbrook, BC, 66
Crimean War, 93, 95
Crocodile Valley, the, 75
Cronje, General Piet,
33, 37, 50–51

D
Daily Express (London),
74
D Battery, Canadian
artillery, 83
D Company, RCR, 15,
18, 44, 46
Damant's Horse, 110
Dawn of Majuba Day,
51
De Aar, 26–27, 62
Delagoa Bay Railroad,
83
Department of Militia
and Defence, 14
Deslauriers, Private Ted,
20–21, 23
disease
human, 43, 98, 129–30
of horses, 69
Distinguished Conduct
Medal, 91, 116, 118, 123
Distinguished Service
Order, 91, 125
Douglas, 30
Drakensberg hills, 102
Driekuil, 109, 111
Drury, Lieutenant-
Colonel Charles, 55
Duke of Cornwall's
Light Infantry, 37, 43
Durban, 102

E
E Company, RCR, 15,
44, 46
equipment, military,
15–16

Evans, Lieutenant-
Colonel Thomas, 54,
85, 88, 90, 105, 107,
110–11, 113–14
Evans, Private, 113–14

F
F Company, RCR, 15,
44, 46
Fenian Raids, 65, 117
Findlay, Private James,
17, 20, 35
Forbes, Sarah, 93,
99–101
Fortescue, Eleanor, 101
Fort Steele, BC, 66
Fourie, General
Joachim, 85, 88
Frederikstad, 77

G
Gamsby, "Old George,"
66
G Company, RCR, 15,
44, 46
George V, King, 126
Gordon Highlanders,
28, 46
Gordon, Walter, *alias*
John Gray, 105
Government House,
PEI, 129
Governor General's
Bodyguard, 124
Granby, Que, 118
Graspan, 31
Great Harts River, 109, 110
Great Karroo, the, 58, 59
"Great Trek," the, 12
Griesbach, Private
William, 82
Gun Hill, 34, 41

H
Halifax, NS, 15, 56, 68,
101–102, 118

Index

Index